I0039486

AGEPLAY:
From Diapers to Diplomas

First Edition

Published by The Nazca Plains Corporation
Las Vegas, Nevada
2011

ISBN: 978-1-61098-190-3
Ebook: 978-1-61098-191-0

Published by

The Nazca Plains Corporation ®
4640 Paradise Rd, Suite 141
Las Vegas NV 89109-8000

© 2011 by The Nazca Plains Corporation. All rights reserved.
No part of this work may be reproduced or utilized in any form or by any means, electronic or mechanical, including photocopying, microfilm, and recording, or by any information storage and retrieval system, without permission in writing from the publisher. Printed in the United States of America.

Cover Photographer, Ben
Cover Models, Rockr and Gaby
Art Director, Blake Stephens

Disclaimer

Please note that this is a book for adults only.

If you are under 18, please find appropriate reference materials for your age.

This book depicts sexual situations between consenting adults who role-play.

Acknowledgements

Good things rarely happen because of only one person. I would like to thank all of those that spoke with me, took surveys, or let me interview them for this book. I would especially like to thank those that helped me with the editing process, listened to me rant, gave me suggestions, encouraged me, or tolerated me pontificating over some aspect of ageplay.

It has taken a lot of effort to get this book together. I would like to thank several folks for contributing their photos to illustrate concepts in the book: MisBehavingMegan, Jyf, SilverPlatedFrog and Sarah Gregory (Ms. Gregory is a professional model and her links are in the *Resources* section). I would like to thank Katie S. for providing a hot fantasy as an introduction to one of the sections, Samantha who took the time and effort to edit this book into something readable, and my ageplay partners for having me explore different areas, especially Violet. Special thanks go to the Leather Archive Museum for letting me examine their wonderfully collected and archived ageplay materials.

I would also like to thank you, dear reader, for purchasing this book. Although this book is the product of passion and a desire to educate, the proceeds will allow me to subsidize my travel expenses for ageplay classes that I teach, as well as attending ageplay events in order to try to reach new people and help others explore their fantasies. I am also happy that you have decided to learn a bit more about this topic and possibly explore your interest in it.

I would like to dedicate this book to all of the wonderful people that I have met though ageplay munches, online discussions, and play parties, and to the many more that I hope to meet in the future.

AGEPLAY:

From Diapers to Diplomas

First Edition

Paul Rulof

Contents

Foreword

Coming out of my shell, embracing who I really am, and coming to grips with my kinky side took me quite a while and a lot of self-searching. At first, I thought I was an outsider and only shared some interests with other kinky folks. Eventually, I got braver and started to tell folks that I am into ageplay. Since then, I have met many folks who, only once I tell them that I am interested in ageplay, tell me excitedly that they are into ageplay too. Some then say that they have always been afraid or reluctant to share their interests or act upon them.

One of my goals for this book is to empower others to explore their fantasies in a safe, enjoyable manner. I have seen so many people satisfied when they finally get a chance to act out their fantasies or just run around in a child-like state. Although sometimes misunderstood, I also want to validate that these types of fantasies are legitimate, and oftentimes, just plain hot. They are not shameful at all. After all, I have encountered a large number of people who share similar thoughts and fetishes. This book will share my thoughts and experiences with ageplay, tips or stories picked up from others, as well as academic insights that may help us understand ageplay a bit better. If you are curious about ageplay or think you may enjoy it, I hope that this book empowers you to try it sometime. If you know that you are into ageplay, I hope that this book gives you fuel for your fantasies.

Finally, I would also like to encourage others who might have an interest or know that they have an interest in ageplay to get to know others in the ageplay community. Overall, the people that I've met through ageplay have been wonderful friends and darling play partners. Go to munches, join groups, throw parties. Despite differences in ideals, geography, or play styles, we are a community. Now more than ever, ageplay is becoming a more accepted and welcomed kink in many different venues. Classes on ageplay are being held, munches are growing in number, and conventions are having little's rooms and parties.

This book offers examples and guidelines. I cannot tell you how to play. Playing is so individual that the suggestions that I offer in this book are simply one approach to doing things. Feel free to do what makes you feel happy. At certain points, you will have different views than what I present, the people I interviewed, or the sources that I cite. That is good; different viewpoints and interests are what makes this community diverse and vibrant.

In addition, some sections use using particular pronouns or randomly assigned genders. This is simply for the ease of reading.

What is Ageplay?

Denny always enjoys his playtime with his mommy. He loves playing with blocks and trains, and napping on his mat when he is exhausted. However, his favorite times are when he is able to cuddle with his mommy in her bed, clutching his plushie and slowly drifting off to a peaceful sleep.

Ageplay is simply adults who are role-playing being a different age. During ageplay, some people will take on the role of children, while others take on adult or caregiver roles. Ageplay is simply one variation of erotic role-play. Many books recommend role-playing in the bedroom to spice things up, and the dynamics of ageplay are arousing to a large number of people. Ageplay spans a spectrum from as simple as the typical student/teacher role-play that so many people have done, to people acting as babies for extended periods of time. People dabble in ageplay and then play on this spectrum to the level at which they feel comfortable.

Types of Changes Ageplayers Adopt

Ageplay involves taking on aspects of children or adults. There are several different ways that people can role-play these aspects:

- Physically – People can role-play by changing how they dress, how they look, and their mannerisms or behaviors

- Mentally – People can role-play by thinking simply, choosing not to understand higher concepts at the time, and using simple language

- Emotionally – People can role-play by having a child-like enthusiasm, indulging in emotions easily and reacting to situations without the emotional barriers that adults have in place

Others aspects of ageplay include role-playing either as adults or caregivers and interacting with the adults that are playing children. These caregivers can be enforcers, disciplinarians, loving or caring parents, or creepy strangers. Through role-play, these adults can try on different personality traits, different behaviors, different emotions, different responses, and relate to their partners in a different manner than they usually do.

Although typically classified as a single kink or fetish, ageplay is comprised of several different spectrums. Where individuals fall on these spectrums can vastly change the type of play that they do and the style that they ageplay. This next section will look at these spectrums more closely.

The Ageplay Spectrums

People can locate themselves on each one of these spectrums according to their interests and desires. Most people will fall somewhere in the middle of these spectrums. Changes in desires and interests can vary over time and with different partners. These spectrums intersect to describe your ageplay style.

Only Casual Intensity   vs.   Only Lifestyle Intensity

←   →

Only Symbolic Roles   vs.   Only Literal Roles

←   →

Only Sexual Ageplay   vs.   Only Nonsexual Ageplay

←   →

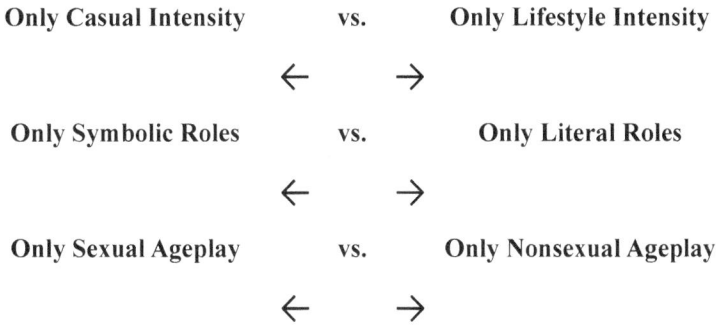

Intensity Spectrum

> *Even though she is in college now, Denise's boyfriend Benjamin loves it when she dresses up in her cheerleader uniform from high school. They have done several different role-plays where he is her high school boyfriend, or in other cases, a teacher. They both enjoy it. He sometimes tells his friends about it and they think it is hot.*

The depth of relationships refers to the dedication and familiarity that play partners have with each other and the level of intensity with which they take on their roles. Ageplay roles and relationships can range greatly in depth. At the extremes, some individuals prefer casual scenes, which involve fleeting and temporary relationships or interactions. Other individuals have highly structured ageplay roles and relationships that are ongoing and not just isolated scenes. Most people tend to fall somewhere between these extremes.

- It isn't about me calling someone "Daddy" only while we're having sex and that's it. If I'm compelled to do so, it is because I think of them as my Daddy or Mummy all the time, not just between the sheets or under the bindings.

On one end of the spectrum is the casual ageplayer. For example, many traditional sexual role-plays revolve around ageplay. These can include student/

teacher role-plays, student/principal role-plays, or cheerleader/jock role-plays. Although it is ageplay, many people who engage in this type of behavior don't label it as ageplay and see their behavior simply as normal sexual activity.

- A female friend and I started ageplaying during recess in grade 5. We would switch off. I would play mommy and use baby spoons to feed her pudding or applesauce and let her drink from a bottle. However, the school stopped us because it was not appropriate to play such games. I also got in trouble for trotting and pretending I was a horse!

On the other end of the spectrum are people that live totally immersed in ageplay. Some people spend most of their time engaged in ageplay activities. One example of this is William Winsor, age 54 (Watson, 2005). Winsor considers himself an extreme adult baby; he always appears in public in his baby clothes and utilizes nursery furniture in his home. However, he still drinks beer, performs daily activities of living like shopping by himself, and surfs the internet.

> *"Customers and cashiers stare at the 5-foot-11, 180-pound man, who is dressed in a pink bonnet, pink shorty dress, and white patent leather shoes. Gold heart-shaped earrings twinkle beneath his carefully curled hair. Under his dress, you can see his diaper. He takes his place in line with a carry-all basket full of juice and Gerber Baby Food."*
>
> (Wilson, 2005)

Related to this, people with a fetish towards ageplay related things vary in how much they require ageplay components for sexual satisfaction (Speaker, 1989). This can range from a slight preference for ageplay, to some ageplayers requiring diapers in order to orgasm.

Like most things, the majority of people who realize that they are into ageplay fit somewhere between the two extreme ends of the spectrum. They have an awareness of ageplay, may dress up occasionally, and have a more balanced level of play between time that they ageplay and time they spend as themselves. They also generally play with certain partners or in special places.

Symbolic vs. Literary Spectrum

- My partner and I have characters that we use for it, and it is a lot of fun for us. We get to assume different roles than normal, act in different ways, and it makes many of the same things we do in bed seem brand-new!

- I was an ageplayer years before I even knew what one was, it is just a natural part of me.

It appears that most ageplayers tend to be more towards the symbolic pole of ageplay, although many do take the roles literally as well. Symbolic ageplay manifests itself by using childhood as a comparison to our current or desired personality traits. So, someone who has fun loving, mischievous, or relaxed traits may identify as a six-year-old boy, since six-year-old boys embody many of those traits. They may also be looking for a nurturing, physically close person who would identify as a mother-like figure during play.

Although much of the book speaks about ageplay, the term "play" is not connotative of something trivial or frivolous. Rather, many people take ageplay very seriously. Although most people engage in age-related role-playing, others insist that they are not role-playing and feel that they are engaging their personality in a literal way. Either method is an equally valid way to ageplay.

People who are more towards the literal interpretation end of the spectrum feel they have a facet of their personality that is still a child. Alternately, the literal aspect would be more along the lines of believing that you are, deep down inside still a child. When these people ageplay, they do not consider it play or acting, but rather releasing and focusing on that facet of their personalities for a while. In this case, you would be looking for a caregiver to take care of you for periods of time or in certain circumstances, not just in scenes. To some people, this literal aspect brings up more questions of consent, since if you believe that you are still a child (or some part of you is a child), some believe that you cannot technically consent to some activities. Here are some words from literal ageplayers:

- I ageplay, because I have always felt myself as a little boy! Growing up, I still felt like a kid. Now as an adult, I ageplay to de-stress, and also because it's always been part of who I am. Even as a kid, I would act like a baby and play with diapers.

- I ageplay because there is a facet of who I am that is still a child, that part who never grew up, who desires the nurturing of a Daddy.

- The people at work have not figured out that I am not a grownup.

Sexual vs. Nonsexual Spectrum

Although most ageplayers engage in both sexual and nonsexual play in certain circumstances, there is sometimes tension between the two groups. Both forms of play are valid and satisfying to those that engage in them. Different aspects of sexuality and ageplay will be touched on in more depth in a later section.

What Ageplay Is Not

People frequently misinterpret or misunderstand ageplay and sometimes it is easier to clarify a concept by stating what it is not. Being attracted to individuals of a different age category than the one you are currently in is not ageplay. Intergenerational relationships involve no role-playing. For example, if one was attracted to children, that would not be ageplay, but instead pedophilia. Another example is if one is attracted to people who are typically labeled "MILFs" or "cougars." Once again, this attraction is not ageplay, as there is no role-playing involved. No children are involved with ageplay. Ageplay is simply a kind of erotic role-playing.

In addition, ageplay is not a type of regression therapy. Although some people derive therapeutic aspects from their ageplaying, it is not a formal method for working through issues or trauma. Although some situations sound somewhat negative, ageplay is not pathological in nature and those who engage in it are not lacking in some regard. Now that we have found out what ageplay is and is not, it is time to look at the people who ageplay.

About Ageplay Numbers
& Demographics

Most of the information in this book is qualitative in nature (describing specific qualities), rather than quantitative (dealing with numbers and percentages). When looking at sexual behaviors, it is always difficult to get accurate numbers. This is for several different reasons. First, there is no way to get an information-collecting device, like a survey, out to the whole population. Secondly, people who choose to participate in online communities that deal with certain sexual behaviors have selected in and are at a certain point in acceptance or desire. The actual population is always much higher than the number that are comfortable joining a community. People who join communities are also markedly different from people who choose not to join. Third, people lie, especially about sexual behaviors. Whether it is exaggeration for pride or desire or downplaying sexuality, people are especially prone to distortion on tools that measure sexual behavior. Therefore, quantitative numbers in this instance are problematic and difficult to interpret with any sort of accuracy.

However, Fetlife, a kinky social networking site, does have several different ways that we can examine data on ageplay. We can examine the number of people that claim a fetish for a particular thing, as well as looking at the enrollment in a specific group focused on an ageplay topic. For instance, ageplay is the 51st most popular fetish with 44,942 people interested in it (Fetlife, 2011). That is about 5.7% of all of the people on the site. As Fetlife is only one site, this information is not comprehensive, but is the best available. There is a wide variety of ageplayers. Only some self-identify as ageplayer; others are on other alternate sexuality social networking sites with different focuses, such as diapers.

The information below details selected ageplay related fetishes and number of people who have them on Fetlife (2011). A slight inflation of these numbers may have occurred due to listing multiple similar fetishes (such as Daddy/ boy and Daddy & little boy) on their profile, which were then combined to create these larger, blanket categories. Conversely, these numbers may be also lower than reality due to one listing a general interest, such as "Ageplay," and not listing anything more specific like "sexual ageplay," or vice versa. However, the general trends are of more interest than the actual numbers.

- Daddy & Son Roleplay – 1052 kinksters into and curious

- Daddy & Daughter Roleplay – 37,580 kinksters into and curious

- Daddy & Baby girl Roleplay – 835 kinksters into and curious

- Lesbian Daddy & Son or Daughter Roleplay – 59 kinksters into and curious

- Daddy Dominance – 226 kinksters into and curious

- Mother & Son Roleplay – 566 kinksters into and curious

- Mother & Daughter Roleplay – 332 kinksters into and curious

- Grandpa & Granddaughter Roleplay – 43 kinksters into and curious

- Sexual Ageplay – 114 kinksters into and curious

- Teenage Ageplay – 137 kinksters into and curious

Now we will look at selected ageplay related groups and the number of people who have joined them (Fetlife.com, 2011). Some of these groups were combined with similar groups for ease of presentation. Once again, these numbers may be slightly inflated because individuals could join multiple similar groups, which were then combined. Once again, the general trends are of more interest than the actual numbers.

- Ageplay Adoptions for Adult Littles (1,446 members)

- Nonsexual Ageplay (568 members)

- Incest Role Play (1,575 members)

- Victorian Ageplay (238 members)

There appears to be demographic mismatches in the ageplay community in several different regards. Many people state that there appears to be more males into ageplay than females. Some estimates (such as this one from dpf.com when it was operational) range from a nine males to one female ratio; in any case, the ratios reflect males outnumbering females. These ratios do not count the individuals who identify as transgendered, gender flexible, or asexual. A quick examination of the individuals with the ageplay fetish on Fetlife.com (2011) shows a varied and somewhat balanced composition of the gender of individuals. When people speak of these ratios, they may indeed be speaking more about a mismatch in the number of people who play different roles.

There appears to be more individuals who play little or dependent roles, than who are interested in playing a caregiver role. There appears to be a large number of both women who play younger girls and a large number of men who play baby boys. One ageplayers expressed difficulties with "*finding a mommy play partner. There are too many daddies and not enough mommies.*" I am sure that many people seeking Daddies may disagree.

Another type of mismatch in the population that may occur is that of compatible interests. Only about 13% of ageplayers on Fetlife are interested in ageplay are also interested in diapers. However, those that only subscribe to social networking sites that deal solely with diapers and diaper lovers may also negatively influence this number. This divide between interests, such as diapers, may influence compatibility of partners. Other sites were solicited for data, but no information was forthcoming.

About 3% of those that are into ageplay belong to the Young Ageplayers (18 to 35) group. I believe that this number is artificially low. Likely, there are a much larger number of younger ageplayers; however they may not feel the need to associate within a particular age bracket.

In order to find out more about ageplay, I administered a brief survey through some Fetlife groups. Using their responses, I was able to pull out specific themes. Some of their quotes appear throughout this book (like in the above paragraph); prefaced by a dot. Sixty-one people responded to the survey. This is not a representative sample, but an illustrative one of people from certain groups at a certain time.

Looking Back in Time

Like many personal or sexual things, sadly there is little information available on the history of ageplay. However, there may be some telling indicators and I will piece the history together the best that I can. Since there are many different aspects of ageplay, I will examine several different possibilities. Ageplay likely varies from country to country, based upon societal structure and norms. This discourse largely focuses on ageplay in the United States, Canada, and England.

Examining Childhood

The history of ageplay should likely mirror the history of the social concept of childhood throughout the ages. Jean Jacques Rousseau was an 18th century philosopher who believed that childhood should be a period of sanctuary before the stresses of adult life. Before this distinction, childhood was not separate or treated differently than the rest of life. Children were basically treated as miniature adults (Postman, 1982). Little before this time would have been recognizable as childhood (Kinkaid, 1992).

It also seems unlikely that ageplay occurred prior to the 19th century, since the Industrial Revolution in England consumed much of childhood with factory labor. The Factory Acts in England slowed and finally halted child labor starting in 1802-1878 (Postman, 1982). The stopping of child labor is maybe one of the reasons why people romanticized the Victorian Era.

After children no longer had to labor in factories, the appearance of childhood started to resemble something more recognizable. Children began to occupy their days with school, got their own styles of clothing, and appropriately sized furniture. People created childhood games and childhood as a whole began to develop social norms and acceptance. It was not until the early 1900's that childhood as a social institution permeated all economic levels and became a cultural phenomenon (Postman, 1982).

With the end of World War II in 1945, American culture once again shifted focus towards a traditional nuclear family and traditional gender roles. Women transitioned from wartime jobs and back into the private sphere of the household and related gender roles.

A Short History of Ageplay

As with many things sexual or private, there exists little evidence of ageplay between the societal development of a childhood role and the middle of the twentieth century. The start of the Baby Boom generation may have had an effect on ageplaying, as there was such a large increase of the number of children and a focus on children, their upbringing, and materials related to children. For instance, in 1949 the first disposable diapers were introduced in America.

Although radio shows for children had existed before, children's television shows premiered in the late 1940's and throughout the 1950's. Shows like *Leave it to Beaver* were possible guides for family interactions and dynamics. These shows and similar ones continued to influence people over the decades. They were still impactful to many when they went into syndication.

Some of the material history of ageplay includes pornography. In the 1970's and 1980's, the only way to purchase pornography was either though the US Mail or over the counter at a specialty store. Occasionally in that era, adult stores carried magazines that had a diaper theme in the fetish section. There were several different adult magazines published that included diaper or ageplay related materials. This included: *Rubber Life, Thumb, Adults in Babyland, Nugget,*

Tales from the Crib, The Play Pen, Tales from the Baby Room, Back to Infantile Delights, The Fetish Times, The Advocate, Forum, The Crib Sheet, and *Dominated & Diapered.* A sampling of reviewed publications showed that many pictorials were largely heterosexual in nature.

Active in the 1980's, one of the largest ageplay organizations was the Diaper Pail Fraternity (DPF). Early founders developed a network of contacts and sent out a newsletter. They attempted to hold a national convention, but ended up settling for regional gatherings. At the end of 1991, there were 13 regional coordinators (Diaper Pail Fraternity #62, 1992). Started as solely a homosexual organization, later it was renamed to the Diaper Pail Friends once more women began to join their ranks. As of the end of 1991, DPF's newsletter had a circulation of 157, reportedly half homosexual and half heterosexual (Diaper Pail Fraternity #62, 1992).

One indication of an origin of

"Diaper Pail Fraternity (DPF) is the worlds oldest and the largest organization (by far) in the world devoted to adult babies and diaper lovers. How old is DPF, you may ask? Well, long before the Web, long before Windows, before Mac's, before DOS, almost before the first commercial personal computers were available, there was DPF. Beginning almost 20 years ago, thousands of adult babies and diaper lovers around the globe have been corresponding, meeting, having parties, finding mommies or daddies, falling in love, and forming permanent, life-long relationships – thanks to DPF. Since 1980, well over 15,000 people from all over the world have found happiness with DPF. It is our fondest hope that we can share this with you, too."

ageplay may be the documentation of paraphilic infantilism (or simply infantilism) in the American Psychiatric Association (APA) Diagnostic Manual (American Psychiatric Association, 1980). This was first included in the diagnostic manual in 1980. Distinguishing this disorder was the desire to wear diapers, other than for medical necessity, and/or to be treated as a younger child. In addition, this describes a pattern of adults becoming sexually aroused from objects to which infants are typical exposed. Touching and the physical feelings of objects often took prominence.

These distinguishing characteristics and the label of a disorder may be been partially responsible for the feelings of guilt or shame that some ageplayers feel for a time. The earliest case studies only demonstrate the most extreme behaviors that were observed. Also, relying on self-reports tends to create issues with which reports are actual behaviors and which have fantasy elements embedded within them (Speaker, 1989).

Thus, these published case studies may be qualitatively different from ageplay. Since most ageplayers do not have issues with their fetish and infantalism has been mentioned in only a handful of case studies, this negative labeling may have been one way that society chose to address the issue of adults acting as children. The emergence of these case studies could be influenced by several factors. The identification of these case studies shows the awareness of medical and psychological professionals to those that ageplay. Whether due to the rise of a new wave of ageplayers or simply professionals take note, the timing may indicate some factors that may have contributed to the rise of ageplay.

The earliest of these case studies was published in 1954. In one case, a study describes a man who has been ageplaying since early in the 1900's, although there appears to be some confusion as to whether this is confused due to possible brain trauma (Pandita-Gunawardena, 1990). This case does document custom made, adult-sized baby furniture. Another case describes women with similar behaviors in 1969 (Allen, 1969). Self reports are listed for age players corresponding with and meeting each other via the US Postal Service as far back as 1969 (Speaker, 1989).

In 1993, the Big Babies, Infantilists, and Friends (BBIF) mailing list began. Also in operation was the IRC chat room: DPF's Conferences and Chat Rooms for Adult Babies, Teens, and Diaper Lovers. By 1994, the UseNet group alt.sex.fetish.diapers had already been created and technology had advanced to the point where the first adult baby websites were started. In 1994-1995, several bulletin board services were created focused solely on adult babies or diaper lovers. Several mail order services catered to the diaper needs of adult babies, as well as several places offering adult baby related publications. In 1992-1993 several talk shows aired with adult baby themes. These included Jerry Springer and Montel Williams. This exposure was one of the first larger viewings of people who live an ageplay lifestyle.

With the spread and accessibility of the internet in the later 1990's and on, groups and sites began to be dedicated to specific interests, including age play and diaper fetishes, and slowly communities were formed. Along with other websites, users started their own groups and communities to communicate with other ageplayers, as well as sharing information and resources.

After having looked at some of the historical elements behind childhood and ageplay, we will now examine some of the reasons that people engage in ageplay.

Why Do We Ageplay?

Rebecca loved the preparations for her scenes with Joy. She felt that it was really one of the few times that she could take time to care for herself and make herself feel beautiful. After taking a long, hot shower and shaving, Rebecca loved the attention that she gave herself while drying off, dressing in the frilly dress that Joy loves her to wear, braiding her hair and not having to worry about makeup. As she took a moment to compose herself and collect her thoughts, she felt the stresses and hassles of her daily work and life melt away, and she felt Rebe, her eight-year-old self rise. She is filled with feelings of happiness, and an urge to play and have fun. She opened the door, ran out, and gave a powerful hug to Joy, all while yelling, "Mommy!"

There are many different reasons that people might feel joy or satisfaction while doing ageplay. The reasons for this are complex and varied. They would change whether the person was playing an adult or a little. Reasons for ageplay include both sexual and nonsexual gratification for most people. This section will look into some of the possible reasons that ageplay turns individuals on.

Nonsexual Reasons

Many of the reasons that people ageplay are completely nonsexual. Ageplaying tends to meet emotional or psychological needs for a majority of people. There are numerous different reasons that ageplay is nonsexually satisfying to people. We'll examine some of these in-depth.

Reliving Childhood

- I want to be myself again, at 14. The kind of person who believes in signs.

A great number of people have experienced childhoods that they look back upon as desirable or ideal times. Especially when focusing on vivid memories, fun times, and play, childhood seems almost ideal. Most often when we think about childhood, the confusion and pain that we had experienced are minimized (Greene, 2001). While adult life can be full of boredom and compromise, childhood was always filled with exciting times and doing whatever you felt like. Childhood also represents a chapter in our lives that is now locked away and that we cannot reenter except through role-play. Thoughts about childhood are filled with powerful emotions and memories. Children often have privileges as well as a positive attitude towards life (Greene, 2001). Many people long to connect or reconnect with those feelings.

Rewriting Childhood

- "At age 4 ½, my baby brother was born. I remember my mother diapering him and giving him much of the attention that, previous to his birth, had gone to me. I guess that I was jealous…and began to have fantasies about wearing diapers." (Speaker, 1989).

For littles, rewriting or re-envisioning their childhood is one reason that ageplay might be appealing. However, ageplay is not simply a reaction to one's own childhood events. Some ageplayers' own personal childhood or possible negative events may not influence their play much or at all. There are multitudes of reasons that people ageplay. Adults look back upon childhood with rose-colored goggles. We forget the confusion and pain of childhood and instead, focus on our lost self, a sense of adventure, and the possibilities of the world that we have been exiled from.

Everyone has something in their childhood that they would like to change: disappointments, lacks, incompletion, and missed opportunities. Some individuals may have had a less than ideal or unhappy childhood (Speaker, 1989). For example, some individuals suffered from illnesses that sapped away their childhood, were forced to grow and become responsible early due to family situations, or want to envision a childhood free of distressing events such as divorce.

Everyone has some sort of unfinished business or unresolved issues from childhood. These are widespread and can include such things as disappointment, painful or awkward memories, and the lack of objects, people, or emotions. Ageplayers may be able to act out and emotionally resolve these issues from their past using play (Greene, 2001). By utilizing ageplay, the individual may be able to "rewrite" or imagine a happier childhood. Some ageplayers tell about why they participate in ageplay and their personal experiences:

> *When I was five, my little brother was born. That's when the attention shifted from me over to him. Besides losing the attention from my parents, I was also given more responsibilities and expected to help around the house. So, I think that since then, I just wanted to go back to being a baby.*

- When I was growing up, I was not able to have a typical childhood. As an ageplayer, I can explore my feelings as a little girl and fully realize what I should have had as a child.

- I am the oldest and always had sisters to take care of. Sometimes it feels like I was never a kid.

- At age 5, I started ageplaying. I watched my mother diaper my brother and liked the fact that she was diapering him. I wanted to be diapered by her again.

- All I really have are theories on just why I need ageplay and why I find it as essential and rewarding as I do. I grew up in a very abusive household, so often I retreated to my room, which—at the time— was the epitome of girliness. My parents divorced when I was eight, leaving the door wide open for Daddy issues, as well as for me to try and struggle to find a way to handle and compartmentalize the abuse. I felt safe with my blankies, dolls and pretty things, and I felt safe around other adults and relatives who I knew had only my best interest and well-being at heart. I longed for this. As I got older, and even after many years of therapy, I still felt like a vulnerable little girl under my tough Big Girl persona. I tried to be as independent as possible as I was afraid of needing anyone too much and the risk of loss that brings, but this only ended up hurting me more as I got older.

- I did not have a particularly good childhood; I no longer did things like celebrate holidays or other things that kids did like: crafts, watch cartoons. Ageplay lets me try to see what a normal childhood would have been like.

- I am letting my inner child free in a way, doing stuff that kids should be doing at my little's age and experiencing things that I didn't get to when I was that age biologically.

- I ageplay because I was traumatized at age three, so I go back to age two and I'm not scared or afraid anymore. I am just a happy baby, not a care in the world.

Ageplaying a more ideal childhood than the one you had would be a way to experience joy and satisfaction from these interactions and provide happier thoughts of childhood. Please note that many people experience trauma or difficult issues in childhood and cope in many different ways. Some of them may turn to ageplay; however, many ageplayers have not experienced a negative childhood.

In some ageplay relationships, a certain amount of transference may occur. Transference is the phenomena where feelings are redirected from one person to another. For instance, due to a physical or emotional similarity, such as a father figure, emotions are transferred from one person to another. Therefore, some ageplayers are able to resolve or rewrite past issues with a prominent figure in their lives, even when that figure may no longer be present. Rewriting pleasurable memories to include your partner instead of a parental figure can also be performed (Greene, 2001).

Media often glamorizes childhood.   The version of childhood that many people experience is drastically different from childhood portrayed though traditional media sources. Media socializes us to expect things to be as we see them in television or in the movies. Oftentimes, childhood is less exciting or more depressing than these media portrayals. Ageplay, for some people, is an attempt at creating an idealized childhood that the media portrays.

Furthermore, many media sources depict a different type of family life than many people experience. Many of the reruns that people in their 20's, 30's, and 40's grew up with depict the traditional nuclear family of a mother, father, and children. A large number of children do not grow up in a nuclear family. Forming families in ageplay relationships could possibly provide the family structure that was always wanted.

In addition, the bonds between parents and children may be weaker than bonds shown in different media venues. This could be due to a number of different factors including divorce, illness, mixed or combined families, work obligations, caregiving needs, abuse or neglect, and many other reasons. Some people may expect familial bonds on par with what they observe through media, without considering these commonplace issues.

Most media (such as sitcoms, stories and fairy tales) that is consumed focuses upon some sort of moral or lesson that one learns. This type of quick resolution is not necessarily realistic, but may lead to a tendency for individuals to role-play scenes with a clear, linear timeline or dealing with a single issue. Some scenes impart a moral lesson or physical punishment to reinforce the message of the scene, similar to media. For instance:

> *Heather simply could not learn how to pick up after herself and clean her room. I've told her time and time again, but she just can't manage to do it. Walking into her apartment, I see the piles of clothes on the bedroom floor and dirty dishes all around. "Heather Anne…" Her head peeks around the corner with excitement, but also a bit of worry as she notices the tone of my voice. "Yes, Daddy?" she calls back. I drape my coat over the sofa and then sit down, shaking my head. With disapproval*

> *in my voice, I call out, "Heather Anne, I've told you to*
> *keep this place cleaner. I don't want my little girl living*
> *in a pig sty." I tug on her arm and she takes position over*
> *my lap. Flipping her skirt up and her panties down, my*
> *flat hand strikes her bare buttocks repeatedly. After a*
> *while and some crying out, she's allowed to get up, and*
> *pulls her white cotton panties over her freshly reddened*
> *bottom. "I...I'm sorry, Daddy," she stammers, "I'll try*
> *to be better about it." I get up. "You will baby doll,*
> *regardless of how many reminders it takes".*

The above scene consists of caregiver figure confronting the little about something naughty that they've done. The punishment (negative reinforcement) included verbal scolding and then moved onto a physical punishment (in this case spanking). Finally, there was time for recovery from the punishment and then cuddling and reassurance that they learned the lesson and that the caregiver still loves or cares for them.

Practicing Caregiving

When caregivers play, they are able to explore the naturally ingrained caregiving traits that they have. They may also practice these skills and work on new caregiving skill sets to test themselves or practice caring for real biological children or other dependent figures. It also just generally feels good for many people to care for and take care of others.

Exploring Gendered Childhoods

- As I am transsexual, it allows me to experience things I was not able to as a child, due to being the wrong sex.

Especially for transgendered individuals, ageplay provides opportunities to explore childhood experiences as the gender with which they feel more closely associated with and different than their biological sex. Through this process, male to female transsexuals or people who are into forced feminization can have tea parties or play dress up without judgment. Female to male transsexuals can be a bullies, have a first date as boys, or participate in locker room towel snapping and embarrassment.

Gender flexible individuals can also explore tasks and situations that are more traditional for the opposite gender. They are also free to mix and match gendered interactions or activities to match their own personal preferences. Once again, they can explore and experience without the sense of risk or being ostracized that may be present in ordinary life.

Taking Different Options

Some people enjoy using age play to rewrite their childhood in order to explore options that they did not take. For example, "good girls" can be teases, tramps, or hang out with the "wrong type of guys." Some other scenarios could include strangers luring children away with candy or experience being good and highly praised for being obedient. Exploring different personality aspects and seeing how different choices can affect us can be fascinating. Some people may have regrets or wonder about the effects that different behaviors produce; using ageplay, you can experience these behaviors and their results for short amounts of time. Through role-play, we can explore this other side of ourselves without fear of punishment or other repercussions (Greene, 2001). Some of the different archetypes that individuals may want to try out include goody two shoes, goth/emo, or troublemaker, amongst others.

Shrinking Childhoods

The traits that we associate with age are not constant; they vary across different societies and across different times. In a phenomenon called "age compression," children are growing out of toys at an earlier age and are transitioning more to consumer electronics (Zimmerman, 2010). For instance, dolls are seen as more appropriate toys for seven to nine-year-old girls, whereas in the past, girls as old as 13 have been interested in them. A similar shift in boy toys is also logical, with the increase in the number of electronics and games that interest boys. There has been a shift from utilizing the imagination or toys to adult concepts of electronics and media icons.

Not only do social forces contribute to this compression of childhood, physical issues do as well. Children are maturing at an earlier rate, which is due to several different causes. Puberty, generally seen as a rite of passage, can end childhood early for some as they mature and move on from childhood activities.

Children from an early age are scolded and encouraged to act mature. For example, children are guided to act like "big girls and boys" and not like babies. They do not always getting the chance to revel in the stress-free nature of childhood. Ageplay may offer a second chance to engage in activities at this level.

The compression of childhood may lead to people later feeling that they have missed some of the opportunities and experiences that childhood has to offer. For example, by migrating to consumer electronics, people may feel that they have skipped on some of the imaginative aspects of simpler toys, such as blocks, dolls, or other toys that utilize make believe or pretend. In addition, by having a quicker onset of puberty, some people may feel that they have missed out on some of the innocence of childhood.

Innocence

- I get to feel the innocence; otherwise, I keep it bottled up inside of me. If I am with my partner, I also feel secure and nurtured.

- I do it because it is a way for me to my little side out and to get some fulfillment of what was missed during bio-childhood, namely innocence.

Maturity is often a troubling concept for people. Without stringent rites of passage, there could be uncertainty regarding when one is considered an adult. Also, the loss of a childlike innocence and becoming jaded with the world seems to be a reoccurring theme with some ageplayers. The realization that there are not magical places, fanciful creatures, and happy endings is difficult for some to accept. The desire to regain innocence and escape adult responsibilities could factor in to a desire for ageplay (Speaker, 1989).

Relaxing and Enjoyable

In addition, ageplay is simply fun. Childhood was a time when you could shrug off the worries and stresses of everyday life. Ageplay allows you to journey back to when play and socialization were your primary task in life. You do not need to worry about what your next meal is, when your rent/house payment is due, or when you need to show up for work. Just relax, indulge and do whatever you feel like. Ageplay can also be an excellent mechanism for stress relief and avoiding responsibilities for a time. Ageplayers articulate some of these the benefits that they get from ageplay:

- It helps me to escape and/or cope with the stresses of adult life.

- I love being free and easy with very little responsibility. Ageplay is a huge rush for me and relieves stress from a very demanding stressful occupation

- For me, it's a chance to get away from the responsibility that comes from my day-to-day life. It's a great way to get rid of stress.

- Ageplay or being an adult baby is a way to release tension and stress by, I suppose, returning to a mindset where things are not only simpler but constructed always in my best interest. It allows me to look at the good in the world easily and explore from the perspective of an infant.

- I enjoy regressing back to childhood. Age play is innocent, harmless fun. Anybody can play. No special equipment needed.

- I like it because I find it relaxing. I find it easy to unwind that way. My life is at an apex of stress and insecurity, financially and emotionally so self-soothing with baby things (my blankies and pacifiers and bottles) is one way to keep me from getting upset.

- Regression to "simpler times" and a break from the stressful life of adulthood.

- Sometimes it's just the fun kid in me getting out, having fun.

- I feel relaxed and happy while age regressed.

Sexual Reasons

- "At the time when I started to have wet dreams, I wore diapers to protect the sheets." (Speaker, 1989)

- When I started searching through these feelings as I began to puzzle out my sexuality, certain things became obvious. I felt most like myself with my comforts—be they blankies or certain girly outfits—and combining these with my sexuality made me feel "right." I also gravitate toward older experienced lovers, and there often develops a Daddy or Mummy/lil girl bond even if that is not my specific aim.

The trappings or situations that they experienced during childhood sexually arouse some people. Many times, this is due to reinforcement. Like in the example above, this individual became accustomed to having orgasms while feeling the sensations of diapers around him. In similar circumstances, people become accustomed to becoming sexual aroused with items or circumstances that they used in the earlier in their lives.

A Combination of Popular Fetishes

One of the reasons that ageplay could be popular is because typical ageplaying combines several different of the most popular fetishes. In the top 100 fetishes, age play came in at #51. However, at least three of the components of ageplay were also in the top 100 fetishes. Role-play itself came in at #23, indicating that quite a few people enjoy taking on other roles. Cuddling ranked in at #81, which may also demonstrate a desire for physical intimacy and closeness with partners. Finally, costumes and dress-up ranked #92, showing how much people enjoy this aspect of playing. Other aspects that can be commonly incorporated into ageplay scenes include: Discipline (#8), Hair Pulling (#5), Spanking (#37), and Bare Handed Spanking (#54) (Fetlife.com/fetishes, 2011).

Enhancing Roles

Ageplay presents a different mental framework through which you can with view your partner or others. Ageplay can shift or enhance a power dynamic in a relationship. You can also enhance submission and/or dominance roles through ageplay. People are able to use this shift to create and/or amplify their headspace. For example, some ageplayers tell how ageplay helps enhance their roles:

- It is a nurturing and loving experience for me. Also it allows me to give up control in a negotiated manner, which is really freeing for me sexually (when it's a sexual scene, which is typically a lot of consensual coercion from Daddy).

- The primary reason for my enjoyment of role-playing is "being able to give up the reigns" and lose absolute control, and savor the emotional/physical dependence. This allows me to relax totally, and allows my spinning brain the opportunity to "spin down."

- I also ageplay because it is wonderful to have yet another way to hand my responsibilities over to another, even if only for a short while.

- I'm a little that needs a daddy for cuddles and reassurance, to make me laugh and giggle, just to be there. He is my rock, my shoulder to cry on, he advises and helps me grow.

- I ageplay with my Daddy/Dom because He likes it. I love pleasing Him. I really like it too because He makes me feel safe, cared for, appreciated as His little girl.

- Because I am in charge and I like "making him" do it. We both get sexual satisfaction from it and it leads to further play.

Here is a sample scene that demonstrates that the enhancement of the father and daughter dynamic and roles:

> *Bridget knew that she had to get back home soon or else she would really get it from her father. She had "borrowed" the car to go to a party and had ended up staying longer and having more fun than she thought she would have. It was already late, too late, as she swerved the car down the rapidly brightening roads. Cutting the lights and slowing down as she got near to the house, she slid silently into the driveway. Then*

she slipped out of the car and into the still dark front room. As she closed the door, she spotted the silhouette of her father sitting in his chair. The blood drained from her face. "Young lady, just where in the Hell have you been?" She started to sputter and began to spit out an answer. "You have some serious punishment coming to you." Closing her eyes and knowing, she bent over the sofa and flipped up her skirt.

In this scene, ageplay enhances the scenario by giving the father a legitimate power over the little. In a father/daughter relationship, the father has all of the power, so it eases the work that the dominant has to do to obtain power over the submissive. At the same time, the daughter is used to taking orders from parental figures, so it is easier to be subordinate when placed into a relationship like this one. Some ageplayers comment on how ageplay assists with these roles:

- For me it's sexual but also so much more. It's a chance to feel feminine, innocent, and safe in a strong man's arms.

- My little side is a small part of who I am. I enjoy age regressing with a dominant, adult partner who will take care of me. Additionally, I like to role-play various ages without regression for fun and sexual enjoyment.

- I am just naturally a little girl. I get attention from my Daddy and get to be allowed to be a little girl whenever he allows me to.

- Sometimes it is a great outlet for intimacy or opportunities for comfort; or to feel dependent for a while, and to feel some security in that.

- I am an adult baby. I am submissive and love to be "put back into diapers" as punishment and to be humiliated, sometimes as a sissy baby. I get sexual and emotional pleasure from it.

Filling Psychological Needs

If we look at Maslow's Hierarchy of Needs, a psychological theory, it may provide some insight into some possible cognitive motivations for ageplay (Maslow, 1943). Role-playing with a caregiver can help people experience many different stages of Maslow's theory. Caregivers can provide help with the physiological needs, such as food or breastfeeding and help with changing diapers.

> *The number one thing for me is it takes me back to a time in my life when I was loved unconditionally. I feel a sense of safety and security when I am diapered that is unattainable otherwise.*

Another set of needs according to Maslow's Hierarchy (Maslow, 1943) is that of love and belonging, where in order to move past this stage, one must feel attached and have feelings of intimacy familiarity, affection and acceptance. Ageplaying with others, especially caregivers, can amplify this sense of love and intimacy.

- For me, my desire for ageplay certainly psychological and deals with my parents, especially my mother. I wanted, or needed, to take some control of my own. Everything that I did wasn't good enough for my parents.

Caregivers can also help with safety and security issues, by making sure that littles do not wander off and hold their hand while crossing the street. Some ageplayers comments reflect this sentiment very well:

- I ageplay because it makes me feel safe and content. It makes me forget the day's stress and worries and allows me to me in the moment.

- Safety, comfort, security, more comfort... it's an inherent part of me.

- Peace. Security. The safety of being protected.

Finally, caregivers can assist littles with the esteem stages by telling them they are good little girls and boys and that they have done a fine job with a task or craft project. Praise and encouragement are not always present in everyday life and are reassuring.

For caregivers, there are also plenty of reasons to engage in ageplay. Some people may want to try on a caregiving aspect of their personality. Some people are naturally caring or guiding and this extends into their sexual interactions as well. Guiding, teaching, learning, and giving can all be parts of intimate acts. Some ageplayers talk about motivation for being caregivers:

- I enjoy the idea of having a younger more sexual lady to mentor, lead, guide, and teach the way I want them.

- Helping my partner re-capture a lost sense of innocence – and earning her innermost trust – gives me great satisfaction as a man.

- I started because I found out that my long-time partner had secret fantasies about it. I continue to do so because it reveals new aspects of my lovers to me, as it also reveals new aspects of my own personality.

- I love the combination of control and nurturing but especially the deep intimacy. The feeling of being needed, protective and strong.

- I like feeling like a little girl compared to my big, strong man. It turns me on to know it is a little taboo. I like being his baby, and him being my daddy.

Playing with the Taboo

> Chris looked up at his friend's mother, Charmaine. "Mrs. Bakersfield, I noticed that you hang around a lot when I come over to see Henry. I've noticed that you keep a close eye on us when we're in the pool." Charmaine looked a little anxious and nervous. "I think that you want me," Chris stated matter of factly. Charmaine looked shocked and started to babble a bit, "But...but.. you're so young..." Chris took her hand and started to lead her to the bedroom. She hesitated for a moment, so Chris moved her hand onto his swimsuit. She felt the turgid member underneath the wet fabric. She followed along more willing then, but still silent. Chris could smell the scent of arousal from her. By the time the bedroom door closed, Chris was already thinking of what he was going to do to his friend's mother.

We all want forbidden things (Greene, 2001). For both caregivers and littles, intergenerational relationships and the sexual agency of children are often considered topics that have been traditionally seen as taboo. The feelings of illicitness generated by breaking these cultural norms or taboos can be quite seductive (Greene, 2001). By utilizing ageplay, you can explore certain intergenerational relationships in a safe manner. Some people have regrets that they did not embrace their sexuality at an earlier age or missed some of the traditional aspects of a budding sexuality.

In the above scene, the person playing Chris could be empowered by several different things. These could include being an active force in getting what he wants, feeling empowered by coming onto to someone, taking control of his sexuality, having relations with someone who is more powerful, engaging in a taboo activity, starting sexual experimentation at an earlier age than he did in real life, as well as other possible motivators. Intergenerational relationships were mentioned several times by ageplayers in the survey. Also mentioned was the awareness of the taboo in their play or life:

- It allows me to "get a charge" out of a taboo subject without harming anyone.

- It's a huge turn-on, probably because of societal beliefs of wrongness.

- I love the taboo nature of it, I love feeling small and vulnerable and having someone over me, I love the abandon of it all.

Fetishes

Ageplay also gives a perfect venue for exploring and indulging in other fetishes. Ageplay is an excellent framework for mixing in other fetishes. Here are just a couple examples:

- Impact Play: Children receive spanking from parents, as well as possibly canings from a school authority figure.

- Bondage: This could involve any sort of fantasy game that children play. Large amounts of ageplayers have been tied up during games of cowboys and Indians. Other scenarios could include a captured princess, military games, or playing jail.

- Humiliation: Childhood is often full of embarrassment. There are multiple scenarios where children get picked on, teased, or humiliated. Some examples include wetting themselves, showing themselves off, and having bullies force them do to things.

- Wet and Messy: This can include children playing the mud, in a pool, or lake. Children are often as naturally dirty and wasteful with food, so there are many different scenarios where children can interact with food, such as having a food fight.

Incorporation of almost any other fetish is possible with an ageplay scene. Sometimes utilizing these fetishes in an ageplay context enables people to feel more comfortable, as there is more of a rational storyline behind them. In addition, exploring a fetish from a little's frame of mind may provide fresh perspective, different feelings, or a different experience with the fetish.

After having looked at the positive reasons that cause people to ageplay, we are moving on to examining some of the more negative aspects of ageplay. Stigma is present with a lot of ageplay, for various reasons. The next section will touch on that in more detail.

The Stigma of Ageplay

Some people object to ageplay for several different reasons. People who are not interested or are unsure about ageplay often have more issues with the more sexual elements of play, although people have other issues as well. This section will look at the main causes of stigma and offer some possible solutions for them.

Valuing and Forsaking Childhood

American society is somewhat of a paradox. We cherish the state of childhood, but at the same time we value maturity and push children towards that goal, as demonstrated in prior sections. Those adult individuals who forsake their maturity for several hours through acts like ageplay are looked down upon (somewhat similarly to the "man/child" archetype) as not realizing their full potential within society. At the same time, some individuals may be jealous that ageplayers are able to be secure enough with themselves to revel in the same pleasures and activities that children do.

Several different traits have been identified (Kinkaid, 1992) in relation to qualities that children possess versus those that adults possess. The most common of these are:

- Inexperienced vs. Experienced- Like touching a hot stove, some things need to be experienced in order to be learned. Children lack the time and life experiences to have common sense and know about situations within the world.

- Ignorant vs. Knowledgeable- Many times, parents and other authority figure spout out lines like, "Just wait until you're my age" or "you're not old enough to know better." Children simply have not had the chance to learn the knowledge that many adults possess.

- Low vs. High- Many times, children are seen as the lowest of the low. They are also not taken seriously at times. This could be partially due to this next dichotomy.

- Powerless vs. Powerful- Children are powerless when compared to adults. Adults make the rules, control things, and command children by telling them "Because I said so." As mentioned elsewhere, they are restricted from activities as well as access to services.

- Empty vs. Full- Children are often seen as a blank slate, waiting to be filled. Adults often complain that their brains are so full of things that they forget information. This deals both with knowledge and with the experience traits above.

- Non-Sexual vs. Sexual- This divide between innocence, purity and asexuality has been largely eroticized and is in some aspects fanciful. This duality is generally seen as the dividing line between childhood and adulthood. Since children are not totally pure one moment and soiled and sinful the next, it may be difficult to discern when they enter adulthood.

In today's society, with a lack of clearly defined rites of passage, the lines between children and adults are sometimes blurred. Kinkaid (1992) states that there is a hybrid of adults that possesses many child-like features. He named these individuals "childified adult." The traits of this kind of individual are:

- Doesn't take work seriously, if they work at all

- Doesn't nurture children

- Doesn't have politics

- Doesn't practice religion

- Has no foresight or serious plans

- Has no extended conversations

- Doesn't allude to anything that an 8-year-old wouldn't know

- TV and movies reflect their prevailing values and styles

Although the "childified adult" is not ageplaying, it may explain some of the stigma that ageplayers face. If people look down on these childified adults, they may also look down upon adults that role-play or take on some of the traits of children.

Assumptions of Familiarity

Secondly, some people comment that they could not engage in ageplay or understand ageplayers because they see their own biological children or biological parents when they think of ageplay. This is an incorrect assumption to make. Using these individuals as an example for comparisons is problematic, as both are filled with emotional baggage and assumptions.

Not picturing one's own children while ageplaying might be difficult, as your children are the most vivid examples of childhood and are foremost in your mind. However, ageplay offers a large number of different roles and scenarios that enable your role-play aspects to be far different than anyone that you know.

Ageplayers can utilize other people as a blank canvas to create positive experiences, free from personal baggage or years of interactions. For example, a girl may have been raised largely by her father, who really didn't know how to interact with a little girl. This adult girl might engage in ageplay to explore a different relationship with a father figure, or to engage in more feminine play or activities that she missed.

Ageplay is Not Pedophilia

- Despite what many people think, there is a huge difference between ageplay and the "p" word.

- I am not a pedophile. I have no sexual interest in children. This is the point I feel I need to emphasize most to people outside the ageplay community, as we're often misunderstood.

Thirdly, ageplay is sometimes mistaken for pedophilia, but these are two completely different concepts. To start, ageplay is about role-play between consenting adults. Only consenting adults are participants; no children are involved at all. If there were children involved, it would be an intergenerational relationship, and it would not be considered ageplay.

The "purpose of pedophilia is not to celebrate childhood or display its virtues" (Kinkaid, 1992). Ageplay celebrates childhood, the activities, dress, and rites of passage. Ageplay also celebrates childhood virtues as well: innocence, delightedness, and many others. In ageplay, all activities are consensual and scenes are constructed to provide participants with pleasure, satisfaction, or enjoyment. A noted sex expert, Dan Savage, speaks about role-play:

> *"Adults can safely and ethically explore through fantasy and role-play things that we wouldn't or couldn't do in reality. A nice girl who would never dream of ever actually owning a human being can pretend to own a sex slave without having to forfeit her "nice girl" status; a decent guy who would never commit the crime of rape can pretend to rape a partner with rape fantasies without having to forfeit his "decent guy" status. The same goes for age play." (Savage)*

People use role-playing in a clinical sense to assist people in understanding others' perspectives and imagine how to work though situations. People who enjoy ageplay enjoy the emotions, trappings, and experience of childhood, not biological children themselves.

When asked about difficulties with ageplay, several respondents indicated that some of their biggest difficulties were coping with the perception that ageplay is or is related to pedophilia. There are some examples of the struggles and difficulties that ageplayers face about this perception:

- I'm constantly afraid people will peg me as a pedophile, which I'm NOT.

- The whole "you guys are pedophiles" argument. I find it very annoying that a consensual act between two adults can be compared to a nonconsensual act between a grown adult and a young child who is unable to make a decision.

- My main thing is when people immediately think it is just pedophilia. It is not. That is one thing that I think is the biggest misunderstanding.

- People who consider it too close to pedophilia to even talk about.

- I think it has been the idea that ageplay might have something to do with children. My wife and I raised four children who are through college and married.

This perception affects all of the adult baby and ageplay communities. In our society today, people are hyperaware about childhood sexuality and very concerned about being perceived as being sexual with children.

Ageplay is not any more threatening or deviant than any other type of role-play. Role-plays cannot hurt people and are harmless. It is about imagination, make believe, and does not influence reality. Having one person portraying a minor does not threaten biological children at all. That would be similar to saying that a person portraying a maid in a role-play threatens real domestic workers. It simply does not. Role-playing a scenario is not threatening at all.

Roles are Incongruous

- Acceptance is a major player, where females are concerned. I suspect it has to do with the genetic association of a mother/baby. Whether sexual or not, a female (sorry for the generalization) will look at a person pretending to be a child/baby as wrong. Using something that is meant to feed/bath/apply to a baby...isn't right and quite perverted.

Tying societal interpretations to traditional gender roles happens all throughout society. Separation from these roles is typical perceived as aberrant. While ageplay embraces many gender roles, it also deviates from them as well. While culturally, women can be seen as dependent (when they are little) or nurturing (when they play a mommy role). This can also be true when males act dependently and defy the cultural norms of an active, aggressive male; which can sometimes be the norm with ageplay.

Guilt and Shame

> *"Refuse to put yourself down, no matter what anyone thinks of your tastes. If you are not able to do this, think about consulting a psychotherapist – not about your sexual preference, but about your anxiety associated with disclosing it." The Forum Advisor, p. 70 (Speaker, 1989)*

Because of the reasons listed above, many people feel shame or guilt in regards to their desire to do ageplay. This shame often builds a barrier and causes these thoughts and feelings to remain private. Sometimes guilt also arises, because they feel what they are doing is wrong. This sometimes amplifies the

At first, many people feel shame or disgrace in regards to their desire to do ageplay.

effect, makes it feel more taboo, and causes hesitation about reaching out to others or satisfying these urges. These feelings of guilt and shame seem similar to the way that many people feel when they start sexual exploration. This seems augmented though, as many feel different and set apart from other individuals and do not feel that they have the ability to confide in or share with many other people. In reality, reaching out to others and realizing that there are thriving communities of people with similar interests usually alleviates these feelings of guilt. Here are what some ageplayers have to say about feeling guilty in regards to ageplay:

- I am a minister. When I was a teenager, I felt this was some horribly twisted sin. I studied the Bible on it and could not come up with just WHY it would be sinful. Unfortunately, while I matured out of the "this is twisted and sinful" stage, many people in the church (and out) have not. Even when I challenged them to show me how, using the Bible, it would be sinful and they could not, they never changed their opinions.

- When I was younger, there was a certain guilt factor associated with wanting to wear diapers.

People with guilt or shame also related a cycle of purging themselves of their ageplay props and paraphernalia, in hopes of getting rid of their fetish (Speaker, 1989). This stage was usually followed by a period of time without using before falling back into the pattern of using them again. This cycle often repeats with a degree of frequency.

Secrecy

Other than shame and guilt, some ageplayers find it necessary to be secretive in order to keep other people in the dark about their fetishes. Some ageplayers comment about their behaviors and need for secrecy:

- Balancing my desire to play with others with maintaining my anonymity is by far my biggest challenge. Because of my paranoia about being found out by the wrong person and getting a negative reaction, I feel a lot of stress about keeping diapers and custom baby clothes hidden, and I don't look for daddies and diaper buddies who are located near me. I only meet guys from further away cities.

- Our 8'x8' bedroom is our play space...we live with three roommates, only one who has an idea of what is going on.

- Hiding my diapers, toys, and clothes. I have lived with roommates for seven years. Before that, I was living at home trying to hide the stuff too, as parents love to raid your room to see if you have drugs and stuff.

- The biggest challenges for me have been finding clothing that suits what Daddy and I think I should be wearing, and the fact that I have to keep it hidden.

- Overcoming the idea of the normal world thinking it is something that it is not; especially in my career. I could see many of my clients and employer being horribly offended to know that I was interested in ageplay

- I hid my adult baby stuff, diapers, and pacifiers buried in the backyard in a box.

Although the need for secrecy may enhance feelings of the taboo, it largely seems like a hassle for those involved. Not being able to share something so personal and important can feel stifling and isolating. Several people commented on needing to keep ageplay paraphernalia and props hidden. If these were discovered, the result would not only be embarrassment, as many people would feel if someone else discovered their sexual materials, but it would also entail judgment or possibly explanation.

The Stigma of Ageplay in The Scene

It is one thing to deal with isolated instances of having to explain ageplay to people that discover your interests and do not understand. It is a much larger step that people need to take in order to find their place in the spectrum of alternative sexual practices (aka The Scene). There are several different reasons why ageplay has difficulty being fully accepted into The Scene. Many different ageplayers had mentioned that even they do not feel quite at home within The Scene when questioned about difficulties with ageplay.

- I want acceptance in the mainstream BDSM community. People look at you like you've grown a second head when you tell them you're an inner kid/little. The first time I introduced myself as a baby girl at a munch the first question was, "Like diaper baby girl? Or just baby girl?" as if it would make a difference either way. I was not dressed as a little; I had jeans and a tee shirt on. However, the first thing everyone leapt to was the idea of adult babies, diapers, and how gross they found that.

- The general BDSM community doesn't understand ageplayers and doesn't really try to.

- There's some stigma in the D/s community, I just want to be myself without making others uncomfortable.

- My biggest issue is acceptance from others, even in the BDSM scene. Lack of understanding, disgust with an adult needing to have this type of interest

- Sometimes, having to talk to people who want to know what ageplay is, or thinks it is odd or negative is a challenge. I try to be understanding and positive as I try to explain things, as I would someone who questioned some of my other kinds of play. It hasn't been too often, but it does come up.

The first and main reason is the perception that ageplay is somehow associated with pedophilia. In the kink community, many scenes revolve around forced sexual contact, often called rape play. While rape play and other simulated, forced sexual encounters are perceived as "hot" and part of the scene, ageplay is not. Both rape and pedophilia are crimes. Rape play is modeled after a crime and widely accepted in The Scene. Contrast this with ageplay, especially nonsexual ageplay. Neither has anything to do with pedophilia, but ageplay is still not as widely accepted overall.

In studies, individuals with a kink background were psychologically healthier and often physically healthier than their non-alterative sexuality embracing counterparts (Cross, 2006). Individuals that participate in this kind of kinky activity do not engage in similar behaviors outside of the scene (such as engaging in rape play and then actually participating in rape). Most kinky people utilize appropriate outlets for their energy, playing with other consenting adults.

The Daddy/boy dynamics in the leather scene may be a second reason that ageplay has not gained widespread acceptance in The Scene. The Daddy/boy leather dynamic focuses on training and teaching different kink related skills. Therefore, there might be resistance, since ageplay dynamics could be seen as interfering with, overshadowing, replacing, or competing with the leather Daddy/boy relationships.

Thirdly, some people can perceive some of ageplay, especially non-sexual ageplay, as different from other fetish activities. For example:

- Some who consider it "not real play" because it is too much coddling, not rough enough, or not enough of a mind fuck (e.g. simple story time, as opposed to play that might lead to more intimacy). That said, I focus on where my partner and I are at and savor that.

Seeing someone coloring, napping, and being snuggled in the same place that people are usually tied up with ropes, flogged, or have needles punched through their skin may be very different and feel out of place to some. Ageplay is a legitimate fetish and should be honored as such. In fact, some aspects of ageplay are very similar to other, different fetishes. For example, pacifiers can act as gags and there is a certain element of humiliation to diapers. Many people use the framework of ageplay to explore other fetishes as well.

In recent years though, ageplay has started to be more tolerated and accepted throughout The Scene. Social networking internet sites have allowed ageplayers to befriend others with different fetishes in The Scene. Forward thinking play spaces have hosted classes and parties, all geared towards ageplay. Conventions have added ageplay classes and ageplay dedicated play spaces. Dedicated ageplay conventions now exist. Across the nation, ageplay munches are held and have begun to attract some people from a wider section of The Scene as well.

Next, we will look at some of the many different roles that exist within ageplay.

Different Roles within Ageplay

Because of the role-play involved, when people engage in ageplay, they are able to take on several different types of roles. This section will highlight some of the roles that people choose to play. We will look at dependent roles and caregiver roles, as well as examining different roles for those who play children and adults. Other roles besides the ones listed are possible, but these are the easiest to categorize and most popular roles.

By reading these descriptions, you may be able to identify traits or ideals that will help you identify or solidify your role in ageplay. Many individuals play within an age range or several different roles, so picking out one role is not necessary.

Littles, Babies, Children, and other Dependent Roles

The little role is the foundation of ageplay in general. Because being little encompasses such a wide number of years, they vary widely in terms of behaviors, actions, attitudes and expectations. Many people find that it's better not to tie themselves to a chronological age but instead identify a range of ages that they like to play or else several distinct ages. The next section will examine in more depth about finding out which roles suit you best. Littles are broken down into several wide categories, each having some typical traits. We will examine dependent roles as they occur chronologically.

Babies

> *Luke was lying in the crib, watching a colorful mobile go around and around. The soft, gentle music was lulling him to a happy place and his mind was simply filled with the colors going around and around. Eventually, his Mommy's head poked over the side of the crib and smiled at him. "Lukey,it's time for your bottle!" A smile appeared on his face and he opened up his mouth, waiting for the bottle.*

Babies are children that are under the age of one (Slentz, 2001). Typically, they perceived as helpless, and generally as passive. However, they are able to get into trouble and can be quite vocal at time. They are also the most self-absorbed, since they know little beyond their body and have little experience with the environment. Babies typically appear in diapers, require a large amount of care, feeding and attention. Typical scenes for this group involve feeding (via either breast or bottle), diapering and getting ready for bed. Here's how some ageplayers describe their baby identity:

- *I'm usually around 12 months but I act slightly younger in some ways. How I figured it out was by looking up child development along with the activities, with which I identify, and found a match. As far as gender goes, I am pretty sure my main identity is male, but I do sometimes have a little girl side that came to me through a series of dreams.*

- *I am myself. But "myself" has been put back in diapers and has lost control.*

Toddlers

> *Trevor was walking by himself now. His steps were still stumbled and awkward, but he was making it on his own. His Daddy was so proud that lil Trevie was able to walk, but he kept on getting in trouble. He kept on trying to get into things that he shouldn't. Regardless of the redirection that his Daddy provided, Trevie seemed to be insistent upon heading towards forbidden areas and putting himself in danger. There really was no other choice but to spank his padded bottom the next time he went near something bad.*

Toddlers are children that are one to three years of age (Kristine L. Slentz, 2001). Toddlers and younger children have some of the same aspects of babies, in that they still may need diapers or assistance with the daily tasks associated with living.

Toddlers have a distinct set of traits that vary with their age; however, these age-related traits may not be closely adhered to by ageplayers. This includes: being able to walk (however, they have a tendency to fall), going through teething, climbing on furniture, drinking from a cup, using spoons, building small towers of blocks, saying "NO" and having a vocabulary of 10-350 words; being toilet trained during the day, throwing temper tantrums, having a favorite blanket or toy, sucking their thumb, being able to undress self, being able to put on simple clothes, and believing that all possessions are theirs (Kristine L. Slentz, 2001).

This stage is more satisfying to play for some, since there is the opportunity to be more vocal with words, more ability to be mobile, and the capability to initiate actions and interactions. Typical scenes can include play, bedtime rituals (such as diapering for the night), and having temper tantrums and then being punished. Due to this mix of babyish traits and the ability for minor autonomy and vocalization, the toddler is a very popular role. Here are some comments from ageplayers talking about their toddler identification:

- *I enjoy being in the toddler stage wearing diapers, being spoon-fed baby food, nursery furnishings and other related things. I also enjoy role-play as a baby girl or gender neutral (despite being biologically a boy).*

- *I identify as a two to two and half-year-old male (the same gender as he is biologically). I have pictures of myself from that time in my life, still in diapers, happy, playing with my Dad and Grandpa. Those photos are my favorite of myself.*

- *I am in terrible twos and enjoy being a bit of a bratty, sissy baby.*

- *I see myself as a little boy between the ages of two to three years old. I have always liked that age.*

- *I have "aged down" to about three or four years old. Since my Daddy is also my Master, the line between my little and my big self is thin and often blurred by the type of play that he and I engage in.. He is more caring, more prone to laugh about my bratty behavior as a little than he is when I'm being "age appropriate." The little side of me has been a factor in my life for a long time, although it wasn't until the last few years that I allowed that side of me to come out overtly or sexually.*

- *I tend to identify as a female toddler. I am currently a female in my 20's. This age just comes naturally to me. It means I can enjoy diapers but still do slightly older things like coloring.*

- *I identify as an 18-24 month old. My love of diapers came before my understanding of ageplay, so diapers are always an integral part. The younger I am made to feel; the more easily I can relinquish control of my adult self.*

- *I identify as a boy, about 18 months to four years old. I tend to be younger (about 18 months to two years depending how I feel at the time).*

Younger Children (Middles)

> *"You get the cookies after you get into the van," said the old man with a crooked smile. Billy was always told not to go anywhere with strangers, but he was just getting in the van. Not actually going anywhere. He was also told never to take candy from strangers, but these were cookies, not candy. Moreover, he was hungry; his mother did not let him eat cookies often. Billy was confused. He looked around and then stepped into the van, munching on a cookie as the door slid closed behind him.*

Younger children (approximately between the ages of four and eight) generally are very trusting and just learning to explore the world outside of the home. They are also mobile and intelligent enough to cause all sorts of trouble. These children are school age and have frequent interactions with adults. These children are also the most afraid of fantasy horror characters, such as witches and monsters. Some possible scenes include playing, school-based scenes, and outings. Here are some ageplayers describing their identification with middles:

- I tend to say I'm a seven-year-old "inner kid." I say seven, because it's old enough to be independent for most things, but still young enough to need help and cuddle without feeling like a baby. I guess my gender when I ageplay is still girl, but a more of a tomboy because I do like playing with army men and things like that sometimes.

- I play a six-year-old girl, although I do still wear diapers and like some aspects of being babied. That is opposite of my biological sex AND sexual preference. I don't know how I came to that conclusion – it just was.

- I am a non-sexual six-year-old little girl, but not a baby girl. I am biologically and mentally female and came to my little age by someone asking the question, "How old are you?" It was in a job interview or something similar, completely not "kink" related. In my head I heard myself say, "I'm six." I will also add that I am more like a tomboy then a prissy girl little, which is similar to how I was in my bio-childhood.

- I identify as a lil girl between the ages of 3 to 6 or 7. I think that was when I felt like it was perfectly okay to be little and didn't know how my family and I fit with the outside perspective of the world. I had my music, dolls, and frilly clothes and lost myself in them when I needed to. I've often theorized that a part of my little must be stuck at that age, but I am comfortable with this and don't feel a need to change it.

- I identify as being between 4-6, and male. I am a brat to my Daddy and also a Daddy's boy (then again a lot of brats tend to see-saw like that). I'm generally a brat to other littles, and come off as very well behaved to Bigs. In turn, I switch with my Daddy, and play submissive Daddy to him when he's in a little mood. He's a horrible little bully :] (this is of course negotiated).

- I role-play as a two to five-year-old girl, but mostly four-years-old. I am in education and I know the ages children develop at, so I knew that my behavior as a little was about four years old. I also suspect that is the last time I felt safe in life.

- I identify as a little girl of around eight to twelve. I am a 24-year-old woman

- I identify as a female (same gender), age six. Even though I have realized I can go a lot younger, still at a potty-trained age, it's just the mannerisms of my little. I realize that her attitudes and the way she behaves are that of a young child, not a baby, and not at all sexually active.

- I identify with a four-year-old. I see being four years of age as an age of some independence, with a bit of control over what happens to me.

Tween

Erin was horny. She snuck into her older sister's room again and turned on her computer. She was so plain and ordinary; her sister had grown into a sexy woman that had caught the eyes of several different boys. She looked at her flat chest and ran her hand over the smooth mound between her legs. She quickly navigated the folders and found the ones that her sister thought that she had hid. She opened one, filled with photos of her sister's full breasts and shots of her pussy that she sent out to strange men over the internet. She was instantly filled with jealousy and resentment towards her sister. Next she opened the folder that she spent so much time thinking about. The screen filled with close-up shots of erect penises. Erin's pussy spasmed and she started to pet it, gently at first, her fingers encountering her wetness at the slightest touch. Her eyes glazed over, looking at all of the hard cocks, the different shapes and sizes, wondering what they would feel like. So deep was her concentration that she did not hear the bedroom door clicking open.

This is an age that is marked by the start of puberty. For boys this is between eight and 14; for girls, between nine and 14 (Kristine L. Slentz, 2001). Bodies and minds undergo many different changes. Puberty is a troubling time for some people and thus a lot of emotion occurs during this period. The start of self-exploration of sexuality and the body also takes place during this phase and is ripe for many different kinds of scenes. Children in this stage have realistic fears that are powered by the media (such as being a crime victim), have realistic job expectations (like wanting to be a veterinarian), are able to see the flawed side of authority figures, have a self-identity, care what they look like and how they're dressed, have a desire to be independent, are able to babysit for younger children, and they may start to catch the eye of their caregivers, classmates or others, and experience puppy love or love (Kristine L. Slentz, 2001).

Scenes can involve typical puberty issues, such as developing quickly or not quickly enough, crushes, and confrontations with caregivers. Due to the start of sexual activity, this stage is ripe for many scenes, especially those of the more sexual variety. Here, ageplayers talk about some of their different roles and thoughts about playing a tween:

- I have two inner-children in me. The first and far more dominant one is a 10-year-old boy that is very sexually promiscuous. While not out and out bratty, he is a bit stubborn and headstrong. The how is far more complicated then I can put here, but the short of it is that in many ways the 10-year-old child had always been there. At one point I gave him the name I wish I had, Brian.

- I play a female, bottom, and her age is undefined, but she has at least started puberty. There was never a lot of thought put into it; it just happened! I was in a subby mood and acting all furtive & coy, and our first scene stemmed from that.

Teens

Heidi planned that tonight would be the night. Her parents were gone and she had the house to herself. Michael was going to come over at 8:00 pm. She had already picked out some music, got her lingerie together, and purchased a new pair of sexy panties that she knew that he would love. She was so looking forward to her first time. She shaved, showered, and cleaned up her room. As the time got closer, she was a little scared and a little unsure in her decision to give herself to him. She knew she loved Michael, but was not sure that it was the right time to do this, what her friends would think or how it would feel.

The teenage years are often ones of exploration of the self-identity, interactions with others, and many different experiences. Many firsts often happen during this time: first kiss, first date, and first romantic partner. There is also a lot of peer pressure and the trials and tribulations surrounding growth or new experiences, as well as the social dynamics of high school and first jobs that often come into play at this stage. Teens oftentimes try out behaviors or are known for behaviors such as: stealing, vandalism, experimenting with drugs, drinking, smoking, having relationships, violating curfew, conflicting with parents, dealing with homework, starting a job, fighting for a right to privacy, struggling with peer pressure, having mood swings, defining or redefining identity or sense of self, being pregnant or having pregnancy scares, purchasing pornography, and making life decisions such as careers or schooling.

Typical scenes at this stage could include having a reputation or being a person with a reputation of a stud or slut, a first date, a pregnancy scare, embarrassment in front of other students, and interactions with parents, friends, significant others, and school figures, such as a principal or sport team members. Here are some ageplayers describing their teenaged identities:

- My age play persona is normally a mouthy, bratty teenager of some sort... it also depends on what all is going on. I have been known to go as young as 7 but as old as 15 in ageplay. I am always a girl – I cannot do being a boy... boys are icky.

- My little girl falls anywhere between the ages of 8 to 16. It depends on how my little girl acts when she comes out to play.

College Students

Spring break, finally! I am not usually the type of girl to do adventurous things, but my friend Samantha convinced me to take a road trip over spring break to Fort Lauderdale. Since I got in the car, I had been excited and scared at the same time. We were having a great day so far. We had met some nice guys at the beach and got invited to this house party. There was a wide mix of people there and I ended up talking to this cool older guy. I had a couple of drinks and was a little tipsy,

> *so when he suggested we go upstairs and mess around,*
> *I was game. We made out for a bit, then he popped a*
> *blue pill and gave me a white one. I quickly swallowed*
> *it down and soon was back into his arms. I guess it was*
> *a bad idea. I passed out after that, and woke up in the*
> *morning, naked, my hair and body encrusted with cum.*

College students are generally typified in one of two different ways: either quiet and sheltered or very wild. Out of control college students typically are looking to be naughty in various different ways through alcohol, illegal drugs, liaisons with teachers or staff, or sexually acting out. Quiet and sheltered students are mousy, studious, and tend to get corrupted or placed in situations where bad things happen to them. Some typical scenes for this age group may involve teachers, sororities/fraternities, or parties. Scenes can also be where college students learn and grow in different ways. For some shy or inexperienced people, many of the scenes that are under this category could be used in a college setting as well.

Geriatric

> *"Well, Mr. Jackson, its bath day," Jackie, his nursing*
> *assistant said. Removing his shirt roughly, she peeled*
> *off the diaper that he was forced to wear ever since*
> *he got to the home. Looking down, she sighed loudly.*
> *"Well, just another dirty mess we have to clean up,*
> *huh?" The once proud banker lowered his eyes and*
> *blushed in shame.*

Although not as frequently found, some individuals like to role-play that they are of a greater age than they are, as well as being a dependent. This type of play may help individuals prepare themselves for growing older or to relate more with elders. Typical scenes for this group may involve activities such as bathing, reminiscing, receiving assistance, grooming, and going for walks in wheelchairs or with walkers. Some hints or tips with this role can include limiting sensory input (with earplugs, etc.) to reflect a loss of hearing or vision and mild bondage

Just as being a baby is reliving my past, geriatric play is experiencing my future.

to restrict movement and range of motion. Some ageplayers in this category go as far as having temporary hair coloring as well.

Whereas most ageplayers cannot usually pass for being their younger counterparts, passing for an older age often gives these ageplayers a sense of pride and/or sexual satisfaction. This could range anywhere from being offered a senior discount, being given extra assistance at the doctor's office with removing clothing, being offered a seat on public transportation, and having their credit card ran for them by the clerk at the store. Here one geriatric ageplayer speaks a bit about his role:

> *I like to pretend that I'm much, much older, like a grandparent or just a creepy old man. I've only played that way a few times. It was a lot of fun though. I told old stories of Canada's past as if I was there, and offered Werther's candies to my granddaughter. "I couldn't have any myself. Not now that I don't have my teeth, but I know how you little ones love your sweets."*

Although a nursing home environment is depressing and oppressive to some, it has the draw of other traumatic incidents or bad things that people eroticize. One geriatric ageplayer spoke about his arousal towards a nursing home type of environment. He conveys that it is similar to "a nursery, where there are helpless individuals under someone else's total control." A nursing home bears more than a passing resemblance to a nursery. The residents inside are often seen as powerless, especially compared to staff. Even when not using actual restraints, nursing homes have aspects that are similar to many fetish components. Instead of a crib, some residents have guardrails on their beds or other functional limitations to keep them less mobile. Sometimes diapers are applied for the ease of the caregiver, regardless if residents need them or not.

One ageplayer that shared that he began to ageplaying in the role of a baby. Eventually, playing as a baby was not physically easy. In addition, after decades of playing, ageplay as a baby also lost its mental novelty as well. Perhaps geriatric ageplay may be a step for some aging ageplayers.

After having looked at some of the more dependent roles of ageplay, we will be moving into the caregiver or big roles.

Caregivers or Bigs

Bigs or Caregivers are often the ones that control many ageplay scenes, set the tone, dole out discipline, control littles, and are generally concerned or in charge. This section will explore some of the different roles for bigs in the ageplay scene. It will also offer hints and suggestions on how to play the role.

Different types of bigs deal with situations in different ways. The masculine and feminine approach to caregiving and dealing with children is often very different. In addition, different family structures and familial roles can influence the style and type of caregiving. Furthermore, bigs in a scene do not necessarily act in the same way as caregivers in the real world. People may be corrupt, manipulative, or overly forceful in the things that they want or behavior correction. The family structure may be idealized and simplified as well.

Mother or Mommy

> *Dan ran into the house, bawling his eyes out. His jeans were torn and a couple of drops of blood were staining the strained fabric on his knee where he had fallen. He clung to her as she consoled him and stroked his hair. Eventually he felt okay enough that she cleaned off the knee, disinfected it, and kissed it. Soon enough, he was running outside again playing as if nothing had happened.*

Mothers are the first bond that gets created after we're born. Thus, this bond tends to be the most powerful (Greene, 2001). Mommies tend to generally have warm, nurturing feelings but be harsh disciplinarians when the time comes and they lose their patience. Mommies typically deal with domestic tasks and child rearing, so they are heavily involved in diapering, breastfeeding, and hygiene (such as bathing). Since they are generally perceived as watching the children and being the primary caregiver, they also tend to be more frustrated with the children.

Women are generally not perceived as being as physically strong as men; however, in this ageplay dynamic that really isn't consequential since a fully grown woman would be stronger than any child. This would enable them to manhandle, spank, and restrain the child as needed. This physical domination by females over males is part of the alluring aspect for some people.

Since many emotions are largely in the female realm, people utilizing the mother role can incorporate them into scenes. Childhood is full of different emotions that have shaped us and influenced us into adulthood. These include emotions such as shame, guilt, embarrassment, and humiliation. Childhood is often full of situations that would evoke these feelings. Some examples of these include being discovered masturbating, being caught in an intimate situation with a boyfriend or girlfriend, having "accidents," and acting immaturely.

Father or Daddy

> *Meghan stormed in the door just a couple steps ahead of her father. Once the door was closed, she spun around, face beet red and crying. She called out, "How could you follow me and Kevin! What about trust? What about my privacy?" The father shook his head. "That boy is a snake. He already had his hands up your skirt and I don't want my baby pregnant." Meghan sobbed some more and venomously spat out her words, "I...love it...I love to be with him!" He shook his head again sadly. "I know, baby doll. I know."*

The father or daddy role is generally that of a strong, male caregiver. There is an interesting dichotomy of both dominance and caring within the father figure. This Daddy Dom role is actually related closely to the Dominant role in many BDSM relationships. With a focus on caring and correction, these aspects are somewhat similar to the shaping, controlling, and correction by the Dominant.

Typically, father figures are seen as strong, both physically and emotionally. The traditional father figure is generally seen as distant and cold, but also caring (Greene, 2001). They are able to take control of a situation and right things. Society also views men as easily accessing their anger and dominance to control a situation, placing them as excellent examples of dominants or those in control of others. One ageplayer who identifies with the Daddy role, Mauricio, states:

> *When I was growing up, I really didn't have a powerful, male authority figure in my life. And perhaps I've missed that. I think that part of my Daddyhood is me trying to compensate for the lack of a father figure in much of my life. On the other hand, I think that another aspect is me trying on the role of a father, supporter, and guardian to those who need help. I think that I want to grow in my caring and be more loving and supportive then my father was to me when I was young. I want to prove to people, although I think mainly to myself, that I can move beyond my upbringing, having learned from past mistakes, and become my own person.*

Many individuals desire a strong, supportive, and caring father who is emotionally close. There could be several different reasons for this. As noted above, in some families, a strong father figure was absent, either due to differences in individual personalities or else because of divorce, death, or other reasons. Male caring is different from the way that females care for children. Perhaps this contrast or a desire to get close to a father figure could be one possible motivation for having this type of relationship.

Fathers are often seen as the ones who inflict discipline and punishment, and often switching to using those concepts as a response. From a scene standpoint, it is entirely believable that a father figure would be dishing out discipline and giving

> *I identify as the adult in all of my ageplay. Sometimes it is more intimate (as a Daddy), other times it is transient (such as a babysitter). Ageplay has always been a caregiver role for me, as opposed to the creepy stranger role.*

punishments. Fathers also seem more in touch with their anger and can be expected to lose control of themselves at times. Mauricio continues:

> *I also think that by having people look to me as such an authority figure, I don't need to worry about overstepping boundaries as much and can relax more in my role. Having the authority of a parent frees things pretty much up assuming other negotiation is taken care of. It's much easier for me to say "Because Daddy says so," and be filled with that parental power and the social system that goes beyond that more so than a lot of other roles. I feel that I have the backing of much of society and more implicit buy-in from a sub when I'm a Daddy-type role.*

Fathers often help to guide children. In relationships that extend beyond isolated scenes, Daddies can use their experience to assist others, guide, give advice, and help littles, especially in tasks related to growing up, like cover letters or resumes, or sorting out school tasks or finances. Some people just need a little motivation or a small push in the right direction to be productive or improve their lives in the way that their Daddy desires.

Fathers can also be protective, someone who we come running to when we've had a scrape or difficulty, as well as someone who we know will embrace us, hold us tight, and help us make things right or feel better. This may influence the aftercare of some scenes, as fathers are sometimes the ones doing the punishment and then consoling the little that things will be all right.

Other Family Members and Acquaintances

> *Jen loved seeing her uncle. He was always a bundle of fun, laughing, joking and doing things that her parents did not. He also always had a gift for her when he saw her. As she got older, she loved to sit on his lap.*

Eventually, she became aware of the hard-on that he got when she was near him. Being the sassy girl that she was, she started to tease him. Grinding her bottom against his hard lap, she giggled and chatted with him. He was staying in her room, but her bed was much more comfortable than the fold out sofa that she was made to sleep on while he was here.

The Mother and Father role are both close, personal roles filled with many emotions and baggage for individuals. People in a scene do not always desire this emotional closeness. Some prefer to play with roles that still have some intimacy and familiarity, but do not carry the sort of weight that those roles do. The roles of other family members, such as godparents, aunts, uncles, and cousins fill this niche quite nicely. Parents of friends and neighbors also satisfy these roles while not being related.

- I usually am a Mommy, Nanny, or Auntie.

The emotional distance, yet some familiarity, often create confusion in littles. Many children are taught to respect other adults and may give some authority to these individuals. However, respect can be twisted and authority may not be legitimate, since these adults don't always care for the children and don't always have their best wishes in mind.

With the rise in popularity of MILFS and Cougars, an increasing number of individuals are interested in this type of role-play as well. This usually involves females taking on the role of an older woman and seducing a male who is generally role-playing a younger age. The seduction, teaching, and intergenerational romance aspects of other types of ageplay are prevalent in these roles.

The Hierarchy of Littles

Aaron and Erin could not stand each other. The feud stemmed from the similarity of their names and went from there. Erin was bigger and older, and always bossed Aaron around. He felt very wimpy and like a sissy

because she was bigger and stronger. It did not help that
she reminded him and all of his friends of that whenever
she could. He could not wait until he was bigger and
stronger, in order to take revenge.

Children often form hierarchies based upon age in real life, and ageplay
can be similar in that aspect as well. Children will often develop bossy tendencies
or pecking orders based on strength, personality, age or other characteristics.
Older children can be put in charge of other littles through tasks of caregiving like
babysitting. The issue of popularity could also be another form of hierarchy that
would cause littles to obey other littles. Charm and social pressure could cause
littles to act or behave in certain ways or do certain things when told or asked.

Professionals

Michelle was full of sweat and scared. She was in the
back of the mall, in the security office, with the security
guard standing and looking down at her. "I didn't take
anything," she said quietly, with a shake in her voice.
The guard rolled his eyes and laughed a little as he
held up the frilly underwear. "Oh, sure. You know, I
hear that everyday sweetheart. All of you kids are the
same; you're all guilty little thieves." He nudged the
underwear and asked, with a smile, "You gonna show
off for your little boyfriend?" Michelle stared down
at the floor as she felt the guard's eyes bore into her
and felt herself turning red, fighting to hold back tears.
He fingered his belt and said, "Well, Miss Sexy, do you
and I want to work this out, or do we need to get your
parents... and the police involved?" Her eyes darted
to his belt, and then to the telephone on the desk. She
closed her eyes and steeled herself for what was going
to happen after she tells the guard her decision.

Actual children are exposed to numerous professionals during their lives, so it only seems natural that littles would encounter professionals while doing scenes. The roles of doctors, teachers, and police officers could all play reoccurring, emotional roles in the life of a little. The role of the professional is also ripe for abuse of power scenarios.

Professionals can interact with littles in several different ways. Doctors can treat them cold and clinically, almost like an object. Police officers and mall security can treat them like a hassle and less than human. Teachers can validate, degrade, or embarrass their students. A nursemaid or governess combines aspects of giving care, as well as being able to utilize strict, disciplinary techniques (Lorelei, 2000)

Strangers

Cindy knew that she shouldn't take rides from strangers, but it was just so cold outside she could not see walking all the way back home from practice. Besides, this guy said he was Kyle's older cousin, and she did like Kyle. Stepping out of the cold, she slid onto the seat, sighing with relief as she closed the door and the warm air surrounded her. He motioned her to a thermos wedged between the seats. She took a sip, and started to cough a bit, then smiled and took a bigger drink. With her head a little fuzzy, she decided that she didn't need to go right home; her mother wasn't off of work for another hour and a half.

Strangers are often seen as a threat to many children. Parents oftentimes warn them away from interacting or trusting strangers, but the unknown and exploration of different possibilities are both alluring. Strangers still capture the imagination, although people that they know cause most (80-95%) kidnappings and sexual assaults on actual children. This concern for strangers could be linked to the fear of the unknown or separation from the family. The fear of stranger abduction is ingrained in many children due to fairy tales like *Hansel and Gretel*, as well as other stories.

The role of the stranger also enables an emotional distance between the people in the scene. For the purpose of the scene, you can imagine that you do not know the other individual, working with a blank slate without the emotional rapport that you usually have with them. This can be freeing for short periods. Stranger roles allow you to focus to solely upon what you want. This could include manipulation, leading, or forcing the little to comply with your desires.

Many people who play stranger roles are generally focused on aspects of being odd people, taking advantage of an opportune moment, or wandering folks who wish harm on those that are powerless. Violence and force is rarely the first option for those many types of stranger roles. Usually, the person in the role of the stranger offers people love, affection, friendship, or a concerned interaction. This can fill a gap or lack in the dependent, especially if parents or caregivers do not offer these types of things (Kinkaid, 1992).

Switching Between Big and Little Roles

- Knowing that my baby girl has made progress in becoming healthier and happier is what I enjoy the most as a Mommy. As a little, it is just feeling the love from my daddy.

Some people engage in multiple roles during different ageplay scenes. They may have an aspect of their personality that identifies more as a caregiver, while another aspect identifies more as a little. Some other possibilities are that they explore different roles as a way to avoid burnout, to experience variety, or because the different roles satisfy different drives for them. For example, if one is a switch, they may enjoy making demands or providing structure that adult roles would provide. Additionally, they may enjoy the freedom that playing a little provides at other times.

Now that we have looked at the different ageplay roles, we will look more closely at the types of relationships that ageplayers have.

Ageplay Relationships

There are three basic types of relationships in ageplay: relationship with the self, relationships with other littles, and relationships with bigs. These different types of relationships share some similar qualities but are largely different from each other overall. This section will examine each of these types of relationships in more detail. This section also includes a description of several different types of ageplay relationships.

Relationships with the Self

Mikey really liked his alone time. When he had the weekend to himself, he liked to shut down the computer, turn off his phone, and lock the doors. He would put on cartoons, lay out some toys, and put himself into a large, layered, comfortable diaper. Very quickly, he'd drift off into his head space, a happy place where nothing outside of his toys and the cartoons mattered. Through

his time in baby space, Mikey has come to realize that
most of the hassles that he had to deal with on a daily
basis were pointless and not to worry about it too much.

For many, ageplay is an opportunity to connect with an aspect of themselves that they have forgotten or set aside. This would include the ability to reconnect with a level of excitement, happiness, and enthusiasm with extraordinary things that we now find commonplace. For instance, a trip out to get ice cream used to be a childhood dream, but now, with the power and control of adults, one can access ice cream almost anytime. This abundant access causes the ice cream to be boring and typical. By examining the simple joys in life that we now take for granted, we can gain a fresh perspective and are able to rediscover wonder in our everyday lives.

On the other hand, some people like to explore alternate models of who they could have been with ageplay. For example, there are some ageplayers who are very sociable and talkative in normal life. One is a teacher and the other is a kink educator. Both women turn very shy and introverted when they ageplay. It is really quite a shocking transformation of personality for these girls.

Exploring alternate personality traits can have two different results. By sampling a personality trait and not liking it, it can reinforce the choices that you have made. For example, maybe sampling being introverted was enough, and you realize that you have a happy, social nature. Secondly, if a personality trait feels good, you can attempt to alter your attitude to fit that trait. For example, if you try on the trait of being peppy, and decide you like it, then you can try incorporating a bit more pep into your everyday personality and feeling the beneficial side effects that it has.

Utilizing self-play, one can often experience headspace as well as possibly learning more about one's self and desires. Many littles find solace and relaxation in self-play, where they engage in littles activities by themselves. Self-play is very rewarding, since you are doing exactly the activities that you want to, at your own pace.

Relationships with Other Littles

Relationships between littles are often important, just like socialization between children is important. Littles can share many different types of relationships, some beneficial and some negative. This section will look at the some different types of relationships that littles have with each other and their dynamics.

Friends

Friendship is the most common bond that littles will share with other littles. Friends can either be friendly, helpful, or mischievous. The role of friends is variable in intensity, from simple playmates to best friends. Levels of friendship are variable, especially in the feelings and actions that one shows another. Most ageplay friends engage primarily in play and socialization with one another.

Enemies and Bullies

Enemies or bullies only have a desire to put the child down, hurt them, or make them feel poorly. Sometimes enemies act subtly, while at other times, they act overtly. Their actions can be mental, physical, emotional, or a mix. Oftentimes, real life friends will take on the bully role in order to get other littles into trouble or to spice things up. This could also include frenemies or brats.

Babysitter

When placing children into positions of responsibility, interesting things can happen. Combining this role with a sibling one also works well. These relationships are often one sided, with the babysitter lording the power over the child, being disinterested in the child, or are caring for the child, the best that they can.

Siblings

- Other than the intense sex, the sibling dynamic is a lot of fun. The banter we have during those scenes is great!

Sibling relationships can have several different dynamics. One way that siblings interact with each other is through adoration. For younger siblings, older siblings can sometimes do no wrong, are idolized, mimicked, and looked at in an ideal light. Other sibling relationships involve a dislike or a hate. Feelings in the middle include competition for attention or privileges, jealousy, and jockeying to be the favorite child.

Relationships with Bigs

- Just that I have gotten very attached to my Daddy and W/we cannot be together as I would like.

Relationships with bigs can encompass a large number of different roles and those roles can have different themes and variances. Children interact with a great number of adults in their everyday lives including teachers, doctors, and family members. Children may act differently around different types of adults. Most roles are somewhat stereotypical and expectations would certainly vary between individuals.

Some of the relationships that people may have in ageplay scenes have a more negative tone to them. This can include some incestuous family members, bullies, strangers, or other individuals who do not have the best intentions for the little. Even though these interactions may have a negative tone, they are still arousing for the participants.

Daddy/daughter

Fathers are seen as the head of the household, domineering, and the disciplinarian. The father daughter relationship is a special one. Fathers treasure their little girls and desire to keep them pure. For example, for many girls their fathers prefer to see them as always little girls and feel a need to protect their daughters, especially in the areas of virtue

"My father thinks I'm still a virgin. When the subject comes into questions, he gets all wild eyed and crazy"

and virginity. Some are especially wary of typical women signs of maturation, such as menstruation.

Fathers can often vary to the extremes of emotion, either being a strict disciplinarian, very lax, or indulgent when it comes to their daughters. They often show more affection towards their daughter than to sons, and having a daughter allows some fathers to be more emotional.   Fathers also provide a source of money for their daughters.

Mommy/daughter

Mothers generally want their daughters to turn out in one of two ways, either exactly like them or else taking the opposite road than the one that they chose. The relationship between mother and daughter can be somewhat adversarial at times. In some instances, the mother wants to be the daughter, reliving their childhood though the daughter, or trying to be best friends.   One type of mother is similar to pageant mothers, who want things better for their children than they had. Oftentimes, social and/or religious motivations play into the mothering role as well.

Daddy/son

The bond between a father and a son is often strong and largely unspoken. The two can engage in various activities including sports, roughhousing, and other "manly" activities. Emotions between men are usually seen as minimal. However, fathers often show a sense of pride in what their sons have accomplished. In many situations, men feel it is more appropriate to discuss sex, make bawdy jokes, and dare others to do something.

Mommy/son

The relationship between a mother and son is sometimes a study in contrasts. Boys can be rough and tumble, while mothers can be caring and nurturing. Boys may also display more emotion around mothers. However, this relationship is a sensitive one, as many sons do not want to be seen as a "Mama's boy."

Strangers

Relationships with strangers are by definition weak and fleeting. However, these relationships can sometimes be spontaneous, surprising, and filled with excitement or danger. Sometimes when one connects or interacts with a stranger, we are unsure of how the interaction should go or where it will end up.

Relationships with Professionals

The relationship with many professionals is cold, business-like, and authoritarian in nature. However, professionals can also have a helpful or congenial attitude, be manipulative, or blatantly abuse their power. These relationships tend to be more fleeting or infrequent than some other formal types of relationships.

Many types of incidents or trauma involving professionals can occur when a child is young. Some people use this sort of role-play to work though the issue or to imagine what scenarios like this would be like. We encounter all sorts of stories of sexual and power issues in the media on almost a daily basis. For example, teachers are being intimate with students, doctors taking advantage of their patients, and statistics on increasing childhood sexuality.

Types of Relationships

Every relationship is different; however most relationships can be classified into several different types, depending on their structure. Regardless of what type of roles are taken on, the formality, frequency or seriousness of the roles that can differentiate them. Once again, having a more serious or structured relationship is not necessarily needed. You should cater the type of relationship that you have to your level of comfort and desire.

More Casual Scenes

During the middle of their spanking scene, Susan suddenly blurted out that "Mommy, but I didn't do anything wrong!" Taking the bait, Rose shouted right back. "You will listen to and respect your mother, little girl!" They both giggled as Rose kept on swatting her.

More casual ageplay scenes usually take place between play partners that are less familiar with each other, are exploring ageplay, or simply when they decide to try a different role. In casual scenes, relationship structure may be light, simply superficial, or else in name only. For instance, one partner may call the other "Daddy," but that relationship would only exist within the scene and have no further ramifications.

Semi-Structured Relationships

The Daddy/daughter dynamic was just one of the ones that Phillip and Angelique had. They also had a dominant/submissive relationship, as well as a puppy/owner dynamic. At times, certain events or things would cause Angelique to break out her little girl persona and Phillip would respond in kind with his Daddy traits.

Semi-structured relationships have intermittent ageplay aspects within them. There could be dedicated ageplay scenes, but spontaneous ageplay reactions could occur as well. While with their partner, people may also slip in and out of roles as it suits them. These interactions could be triggered by something as simple as a situation or watching cartoons, prompting them to delve into their roles for a while.

Structured Relationships

Whenever Brian and Edward got together, they just seemed to fall into their Daddy and boy roles. Brian seems to get more impulsive, while Edward seems to naturally fall into a teaching and explaining mode.

More structured relationships entail many different kinds of situations. Individuals who play together frequently can generate different types of formal ageplay relationships. These individuals have experience playing with each other and likely have some sort of formal role-playing role with each other. This could be siblings, Daddy/daughter, or some other set of roles.

Some couples focus their relationships largely around the ageplay dynamic. This could be by incorporating distinct parts of ageplay into their everyday relationships.

In a more fully integrated style of relationship especially, having ageplay interactions on a daily basis is quite important to reinforce the bonds and roles of the relationship. Additionally, by simply viewing their roles as those of a big and little, one can transcend a scene with these relationship roles. One partner is responsible for bills, guidance, and logistics; while the other deals with fun, playfulness and emotions. There are many things that caregivers can do to facilitate headspace for both themselves and littles. Here are a couple examples:

- Have set chores or a to-do list

- Hold hands or several fingers when crossing the street

- Open the car door and fasten the seatbelt for your little

Now that we have examined some of the different styles of relationships within ageplay, we will be looking at different activities that are common to many ageplay scenes. These activities generally are the basis of scenes for many individuals.

Ageplay Activities

Ageplay can be composed of many different things. This section will identify and explain some of the more popular activities that many people use in age play. Ageplay can encompass many activities above and beyond those listed in this section, as individual preference will vary.

Play

Many ageplayers enjoy engaging in different types of crafts and playful behavior. This could include things like board games, active games (like tag, hide and seek, or red rover), coloring, watching cartoons, playing video games, and building with blocks, Lincoln Logs, and Legos, as well as playing with other toys. Oftentimes, people slip into play mode while listening to music or watching movies, especially as there is little difference in the movies or music marketed to adults and children (Postman, 1982). Using your imagination and creating games or scenarios would also fall under this category. This type of play can either be with one's self or with others.

Lately, the unstructured play of children has practically disappeared. This has been replaced by more structured activities (such as little league teams), replacing informality and joy with structure, rules, and a focus on winning (Postman, 1982). Through ageplay, we can recapture play without structure.

Diapers

- Diapers are a turn-on and they represent a state of submission, as well as a certain degree of sexual excitement and foreplay.

- The diapering/changing ritual always does it for me.

- The diapering process does it for me. Most of the time I diaper myself and within 10 minutes I am there, but when an authority figure (Domme/ Dom) does it, I sink immediately.

Diapers are quite commonly used in ageplay and adult baby scenes, and are quite full of symbolism. Diapers can symbolize a lack of control and immaturity. When we speak about diapers, we're referring to both disposable diapers, as well as cloth diapers and rubber pants to cover those.

- For me, I grew up with cloth diapers and plastic pants. Gerber, Curity, Johnson & Johnson, and all of these products left an imprint in my mind. The sight of, the feel of, and smells of these products to this day I strongly associate with love and security. I feel most secure and comfortable in cloth diapers and plastic pants.

The reasons for having a diaper fetish or using diapers most likely have a couple of different components. The first is physical and sensational. People choose to use diapers in different ways. Some prefer the relative comfort and feeling of the diaper alone, without using it for its intended purpose. Others choose to wet the diaper with urine and/or make a messy diaper with feces. Urine and feces in the diaper produce different physical sensations (Speaker, 1989). Another sensory aspect of utilizing the diaper is the odor or scent of the diaper and excrement after using the diaper. Both urine and feces have a distinct smell. A diaper lover (DL) describes the sensations:

- It is a huge turn-on, probably because of societal beliefs of wrongness.

Some enjoy the taboo feeling of choosing to use a diaper instead of the toilet. Others are aroused by being forced to use a diaper. For still others, it's the sensation of expelling the waste or feeling it in the diaper. Many psychological theories have focused on the trauma of potty training, which may be one reason why so many people are fascinated by it. Through overly strict or overly lax potty training, some theories say that it is a formative event in shaping personality traits, such as if one is messy or neat.

Choosing to neglect potty training and use a diaper during a scene could be indicative of a desire to rewrite part of their personality or explore different aspects, at least temporarily. People who are overly organized (anal-retentive) could relax and revel in their messiness and childishness, and indulge or explore the shame in messing (anal expulsive) aspects for a while.

For a caregiver, diapering and changing diapers is another form of caring and caregiving. Dealing with bodily waste from another person shows a total acceptance for the other person, regardless of what happens. In addition, the cleaning aspects of diapering shows a type of redemption and renewal, by the caregiver making what was dirty clean. From a caregiver perspective:

- The diapering definitely has to do with my control over him. I decide how he's diapered and how long he sits with a wet diaper. He's totally dependent on me for that.

The second is psychological and relates to memories or symbolism of the diaper. This could be feelings of safety, security, and comfort that the individual felt when they were young. Diapers can also evoke a feeling of dependence, waiting on someone else to clean up after biological needs. Using a diaper can also cause feelings of humiliation or shame, as it means having failed at performing toilet training (Speaker, 1989). It depends on the person as to whether this shame is intentionally created or simply a byproduct of the diaper usage.

- I was beaten and humiliated in their attempt to cure me of bedwetting and daytime wetting accidents. I was about 4-years-old when I took a pair of my sister's cloth diapers and plastic pants. I tried putting them on while hiding under the blankets that night just to find my mother was watching when I emerged. This was met with a terrible beating. As I grew older the wetting continued and I was subjected to many forms of discipline as they attempted to cure me. I tried many things in an attempt to not wet the bed. I even took a strap and strapped my penis to my belly as hard as I could in hopes that this would prevent me from wetting the bed during the night. It didn't work either.

- As I have explored my inner child, I have found that being diapered and wetting my diaper during the day seems to have a healing effect on me. To be able to wet with the protection of a diaper, without guilt or fear of punishment, has a very positive effect for me

At first, urinating in front of other people is often difficult, as we are not used it. Just naturally, many individuals have performance anxiety when using the bathroom in front of others. If your little is not comfortable with it, you may want to encourage or force them to drink a large amount along with the diaper play. This will ensure that they will wet their diaper eventually.

Although some people prefer the natural progression of fecal elimination, others are concerned about feeling anxious in regard to being able to eliminate in front of other people. Solving this issue sometimes involves using laxatives or suppositories. The use of these items also increases the feelings of discomfort and an even further loss on control.

Rules, Structure, Boundaries and Discipline

- Speak to and treat your little like they are a real child. You have to be patient and tolerant. Littles will try to make you angry because they want a spanking.

Caregivers should not be hesitant about setting rules and enforcing those rules with discipline. One of the largest desires of many ageplayers is experiencing rules and finding boundaries once again. Being an adult is a freeing experience, and while many rules are in place for adults, many of them are vague boundaries and issues that people rarely run up against (like laws against murder, etc). These rules leave a lot of room for people to get in trouble and not get sanctioned. Do not be afraid to mix together tenderness and punishment. Most children love a little discipline. It makes them feel cared for and secure (Greene, 2001). Adults can buy as much candy as they like, eat as much bacon as they want, and stay up until whatever hour they like. Childhood rules are much closer to the individual and much more practical. Additionally, these rules tend to regulate a lot more behavior.

No cookies before dinner, clean up after yourself, and wash behind your ears are all specific instructions that children get to shape their behavior for ideal living.

One positive to discipline in ageplay, is once the discipline (spanking, etc.) is over, the infraction is done and forgotten. This is unlike real world infractions, which are brought up repeatedly, such as nagging to do chores, a criminal record, or late payments. This is mentally freeing.

"Forced" Age Regression

Along with the forced activities mentioned above, forced regression is a topic that is common in ageplay. Forced regression has the theme of individuals being forced to regress into a younger age, somewhat against their own will. Although they consent to the activity, they are hesitant to experience being turned into a little. Although the below example uses the term baby, one can regress to any age they desire.

For example, people fantasize about a period where they are forced to act like a child, but are still an adult and have their full capacities. This forced regression can include aspects of being made to use diapers, eat baby food, speak or act like a baby, and to have the fact that they are indeed an adult denied. If they speak or behave like an adult, they'll be punished until they begin to act like a little again. Forced regression is somewhat like forced ageplay, but of course, both occur consensually. Being forced to give up all of your adult aspects is different from ageplay, but may be more freely embraced by some, since it is forced and they are not given a choice. Forced regression can instill feelings of helplessness and hopelessness at times. It forces one to need people and their love or caring. Especially when one cannot ask or is not allowed to ask for things, it makes the dependency portion of the relationship key and realizing how much that they require the other person to provide for their needs.

Other "Forced" Activities

Sometimes ageplay scenes can incorporate elements of "forced" activities, such as bedwetting, diaper use, and sexual contact. In reality, these scenes are not forced at all, but rather planned and consented to beforehand. Being forced via role-play to do something, people are being given the opportunity to fight, struggle, be coerced, and be manipulated, to experience feelings of betrayal, feelings of power, and the feeling of violation in an acceptable context. It can be emotionally satisfying for some to feel the dynamic of powerlessness or defeat. Such play does not glorify or encourage forcing people to do things in real life, but much like an actor in a role, allows consenting people to experiment and see the ramifications of their actions. This can force people into experiencing headspace, as well as possibly learning more about one's self and desires.

Erotic Hypnosis and Ageplay

Sometimes erotic hypnosis enables individuals to enhance or more easily slip into their own headspace. Erotic hypnosis sometimes allows people to explore headspace and more easily visualize that they are a little. Erotic hypnosis also allows guided visualizations to be experienced.

Sissification, Cross-dressing & Gender Play

Sissification typically involves aspects of humiliation, dressing in frilly girl clothes, and being made to act like a girl, talk like a girl, and express feminine behaviors. Combining sissificiation with ageplay is an excellent combination. It double disadvantages the sissy by classifying him into two roles that generally are perceived as having less power, that of being feminine and that of being a child, especially when compared to an adult male.

Cross-dressing is similar to ageplay in some regards. Instead of dressing to change your gender, you can dress to change your age. Both are related in that they generally let the person doing them experience a less powerful role, as well as a more desirable one. Both are enjoyable but may also contain an element of humiliation at times.

Historically, infants and children were treated as neuters or asexual beings until a certain age. In addition, many boys were dressed as girls in parts of the world until as late as the end of World War I (Kinkaid, 1992). Dealing with either embracing or ignoring these gender norms through play would allow people to explore their gender identity and the way that how they were treated as they were maturing.

- I play a young child, up to age 6-10, aware of some aspects of sex and the world but doesn't understand much of the world around it. Depending on feelings can be "sexless" (possibly leaning slightly towards one gender or the other), boy or "girl." These roles typically are being treated as a naive and docile child.

Incest Role-play

While ageplaying, some people incorporate incest role-play aspects into their sexual interactions. Since parental and child roles are common in ageplay, this also tends to be the biggest source of sexual play as well. Incest role-play appeals to many ageplayers simply because of its taboo nature and large amount of intimate feelings. Ageplayers surveyed or interviewed did not state that they had actual incestuous thoughts or experiences in regards to their own relatives. Many traditional psychological theories believe that dependent relations with parent are erotically charged, with the child, mother and father in competition for attention of each other (Greene, 2001). Siblings or grandparents may be targets or aggressors in these sorts of relationships as well.

> *I like how much it has turned me on, when my daddy and mommy touch me in naughty places. It is always a special memory.*

Breastfeeding and Lactation

- Being actually breastfed by a partner (she was lactating) is one of my favorite memories.

- My wife woke me in the middle of the night complaining of being painfully engorged with milk and needing relief. That was the most intimate bonding moment; to be diapered, cuddle, and nursing on her was the most amazing thing. I happily did as she asked and nursed long enough to relive her discomfort.

Breastfeeding is an activity where the child is very dependent upon the mother. It could also provide a baby an opportunity to be finicky and demanding. Mimicking breastfeeding is an exciting and bonding experience to some, while others go further and actually induce lactation. This act is very personal, and demonstrates caring and nurturing as one is taking the part of another into them.

Now that we've looked at some activities that people incorporate into ageplay, we'll take a look at how people make these activities into scenes.

Types and Examples of Scenes

Most ageplay interactions are a scene of some sort. The motivation and desire driving an ageplay scene can vary quite a bit. Several different types of scenes exist, all of them depicting different aspects of childhood. Scenes can be spontaneous or heavily negotiated and planned; they can be long or short, inconsequential or heavily emotional.

Play

Jason could have easily bought anything in the toy store when he was himself. But when he was Michael's little boy, he was powerless and broke. He raced up and down the aisles at Toys R Us, throwing possibilities into a cart. Daddy said he could have a toy, now just to pick one. His head spun. His heart raced as he plowed through the possibilities. It was such a struggle, only choosing one, but finally he did. Jason endured what seemed like

a long car ride home. Then he was finally sprawled out
on the floor tearing into the packaging and ripping out
the parts of the toy. His Daddy was lying on the floor
next to him, watching his pure bliss and ready to help
him play with his new toy.

Play scenes are full of fun and joy. These can be as simple as playing with toys, doing crafts, playing games or just running around. The goal of this type of play is simply enjoyment and experiencing fun times. Littles change activities spontaneously and frequently, generally without much ceremony. Children are typically identified with motion, especially when playing. This could include running, jumping, twirling or many other different kinds of activities. While children play, adults typically do not. The ability to play is one of the things that separate children from adults (Kinkaid, 1992). Thus, having play as a component of a scene is naturally child-like.

Bigs can get involved with playing as well, as they color with littles, read stories, play with blocks, or help them do a task. There can also be a bit of structure here, such as guidance with projects and encouraging them to clean up after themselves. Typically, most play scenes are guided by littles and have an overall feeling of equality between littles and bigs.

Punishment

Amber had not done her homework once again and her
mother was not pleased. "Do you know how much we
pay for you to go to that school? And you can't even
be bothered to do your homework?" Shaking her head,
she dragged Amber by her cheek, tears dripping on her
fingers and Amber's pleas in the air. Through Amber's
thrashing, she dragged her onto the back of a chair, bent
her over and pulled down her jeans, showing off her
panties. Pulling out a wooden spoon from the kitchen
drawer, she swung and slammed the spoon into Amber's
buttocks, eliciting another yelp and leaving behind a

large red mark on her pale bottom. After repeated hits,
Amber was sobbing and gasping. "I'll teach you to pay
attention to your classes, girl! Maybe now that you ass
is sore, you'll focus instead of getting more of the same
tomorrow!" Amber nodded her head, throat still sore
from the screeching and crying.

A punishment scene involves administering or receiving some sort of negative circumstance in return for having performed some bad or undesirable behavior. Punishment scenes can either be based on real-life or fictitious infractions. Punishment scenes are generally initiated and controlled by bigs.

In some scenes, people may use the discipline to motivate themselves to perform better in real life on things like eating habits, exercising, or spending issues. This type of play is distinctly different from abuse in that the correction is desired by the person who is being punished. For example, one could negotiate that if a spending limit of $50 per week is set, and $75 is actually spent, the little would receive 25 strokes with the cane to teach them to spend less.

A punishment scene can include several different things. Chiding, scolding, embarrassment (standing in the corner), discomfort (mouth washed out with soap) and physical punishment (such as spanking and caning) are all included in this type of scene. Incorporating punishment into ageplay scenes should be used with a couple of cautions. Remember that while in an ageplay scene, you have taken on a persona that is different from ones used in other types of kinky scenes. Some punishments may have a different effect while in an ageplay headspace. Some people also feel that only age appropriate punishments should be done in ageplay scenes. For example, degrading statements can be taken in or internalized at a much deeper level than in other types of scenes. Sometimes, pain tolerance has been reported to be different from in other types of scenes. This may be a side effect of the childlike headspace that the little is in.

Oftentimes the interactions leading up to the punishment act as a form of foreplay. This could include the lecturing about the deeds, accusing the perpetrator, listing the offenses, sentencing the individual to a punishment, undressing, and the punishment itself. It also seeks to eroticize the power between the individuals (Kinkaid, 1992).

Although punishment scenes may appear to be about distancing the participants with the exercising of the power inherent in the roles, these punishments actually serve to bring the participants closer. The resolution of the offense, and the authority wielded, cement the legitimacy of roles and relationship between the participants. The soothing and aftercare of the punishment is often reassuring and reaffirming for relationships.

Intimate and Sexual Scenes

Amber just wanted to hang out with the popular girls. She was popular in her old school, but when her father had gotten a new job she had to transfer and start at a new school. Now she just wanted to fit in, be popular again and not get picked on. The clique of popular girls had asked her to do a couple of silly, stupid things as kind of an initiation rite. She ate what that they told her to, sassed off to the teachers that they told her to, and dressed how they wanted one day. Now she seemed to be at the final task. Walking into the locker room, she shrugged off her coat, shivering a bit, and placed it into a locker along with her shoes. She shivered again as she lay on the bench, her naked back and buttocks sticking to the cold wood with her nervous sweat. She spread her legs, knowing it would be the first thing the victorious players would see when they entered the locker room. The roar of the crowd outside overwhelmed the clicking of the handcuffs that she used to attach herself to one of the benches. That meant that their football team was winning, so hopefully they would be in a good mood after the game. She knew that she would be popular after this.

Many people find either intimate or sexual scenes satisfying, especially as littles. While in little headspace, many are able to experience sexual play without the related feelings of guilt or any other negative emotional feelings. They simply experience the sensations pleasurably, without the related negative stigma or confusing rules and decisions that some perceive come with sex.

Some ageplayers also enjoy role-playing something that is considered taboo. The forbidden or discouraged is often seen as a challenge or turn-on, and sexuality would certainly be in this area. Many sexual interactions between minors are seen as taboo. Teens worry about getting caught making out, becoming pregnant, or acceptance of their romantic partners. Part of this taboo is the innocence and opening the world of sexuality to someone (Kinkaid, 1992).

An additional possibly for sexual scenes includes connecting in a different way with loved ones. Parents who are physically distant with their children may provoke desires of physical closeness and touch, along with a desire to be wanted in their children. Through role-play, ageplayers can connect with parental surrogates and feel the fulfillment of both physical and emotional closeness.

Scenes or Interactions in Public

> *It was a nice day and Hank and Violet were walking hand in hand heading towards the restaurant for lunch. She was holding onto two of his fingers and he kept her close as they were crossing streets. On the way to the table he grabbed her some crayons and a placemat to color on. She looked at the menu and told him what to order. When the server came, he ordered for both of them while she colored.*

Playing in public is especially emotionally evocative to some, since so many people have harbored shame or guilt about their ageplay fetish. Interactions and outings seem to be some of the most vivid memories for many littles. One of the reasons that these interactions may be so vivid is that you're participating in secret interactions, where you know what's going on, but those around you don't (Greene, 2001).

Some of the ageplayers that were surveyed talked about their favorite scenes being of trips or outings where they interacted with or were near non-ageplayers in an ordinary environment.

- The best is being able to share with a daddy or fellow diaper buddy, especially when traveling a long distance, where all worries about being seen by someone I know disappear. My favorite age play memory is from 10 years ago. I met a Daddy in New Mexico; we spent an entire weekend with me as a 2-year-old. It was just before Christmas, so I got my picture taken with a mall Santa, we went to the zoo, we went out to eat, etc. I was thickly diapered the entire time, and obviously so. Daddy changed me when needed, fed me, bathed me, and played with me. It was pure heaven!

- I enjoy my Daddy taking me places like the zoo and stuff. Playing with my daddy, drawing him pictures, snuggling with him. My favorite memory is when Daddy and I went to the fair, and he bought me cotton candy and a stuffed animal. It was our first daddy/girl outing.

- My favorite memory was watching a fireworks display with Mommy- curled up in blankets, snuggling up to each other. It wasn't a scene as such but I was in little space watching it.

Outings have always been special for children, and for littles it is the same. Outings are enhanced when in littles space, because of the contrast of doing such a private thing (little's play) in the outside world. There's always the concern that someone will notice your behavior. Here are some examples of play in public:

- My favorite memory is when in a CVS pharmacy my Domme asked the stock girl where to find diapers in my size and diaper rash cream. I turn redder than my bottom after a good spanking.

- I get to go to Wal-Mart as an 8-year-old and get my Daddy to buy me a coloring book, crayons, and candy.

However, the outside world is usually oblivious to things that aren't horribly obvious, as people are more often concerned with themselves than other people. Also, many things can be explained away easily. Even if people notice diapers under clothes, many people need diapers for legitimate medical reasons. Holding hands when crossing the street can simply be closeness and affection. You can order food for your little when dining out, and when the food comes, you can cut up meat and prepare the meal for your little. Wetting in a public place could be also be considered a medical issue. For the sake of other deviants and yourself, please be cautious when playing in public spaces as to not draw too much attention to yourself or make it obvious that you're engaging in alternative sexual acts.

Mixed Scenes

I was laying on the floor coloring when Daddy got home today. I was wearing my favorite little skirt, even though it was getting a little too small. Daddy pulled up a chair and sat down behind me. He sat quietly for a bit watching me color. "Katie," he said in a low angry voice. I turned and looked at him, a little worried at what was coming next. "Yes Daddy?"

"I can see your panties, Katie. Little girls shouldn't let boys see their panties," he said. "I'm sorry sir, I'll go change." I got up from the floor and turned to go but he caught my arm and pulled me in front of him.

"You need to be punished first." He lifted my skirt and pulled my panties down slowly. "Open your mouth." I closed my eyes and opened my mouth. I could feel the silky fabric of my panties in the back of my throat as he stuffed them in my mouth. He pulled me down over his lap and his warm hand slid up my leg. I knew what was coming next. I tried to say I was sorry again but the only thing that came out was a muffled yelp after the first smack hit my ass. Again and again he spanked me until I could feel the heat on my skin. Daddy's fingers felt me after a particularly firm whack and he could tell that I was enjoying my punishment a bit too much.

'On your knees." Daddy said it low and slow, so I knew this punishment was not over. He stood so his bulge was at eye level. He pulled the panties from my mouth and held them to my face, so close I could smell my scent wafting from them. "I don't think you understand what happens to boys when they see you in these."

"Yes sir, I do understand," I whispered softly with my eyes to the ground. I felt his firm hand grasp my jaw. I nodded yes, unable to respond any other way. He patted my head softly. "I'm glad you have learned your lesson little girl."

Of course, most scenes incorporate some examples from each of the above sections. It is common for one type of scene to transition or add elements of another type of scene. A fun playful attitude without regard for the rules can generate a punishment. Littles choosing to play instead of doing chores would generate punishment from an authority figure. Playing with an adult figure could devolve into sexual play. The opportunities are endless.

Power Dynamics in Ageplay
Scenes and Relationships

- Being under control of another and dependent is what really turns me
  on.

Although dominance and submission isn't always part of ageplay, there
certainly are power dynamics in many ageplay scenes. There is a power imbalance
in almost every sexual relationship (Kinkaid, 1992). Since many scenes mimic or
simulate real life situations, power dynamics are quite important. In this section,
we'll look at different forms of dominance and control in ageplay scenes.

Bigs in Control

*Bianca was tipsy, just the way that she liked to be. After
a couple of cosmos, she was feeling just about right.
Michael, the boy who cuts her grass, was very tipsy. She
had seen the way that Michael had looked at her, lustily,*

whenever she gave him his money. It was especially hot and she invited Michael in and gave him a drink. Although she was sure that he didn't need it, the drink made him especially compliant. He was willing, eager, young, and ready. It's just what she needed. He loved it, and she looked forward to him cutting the grass more often.

Naturally, there is a great disparity in power between children and adults. Just like in real life, most often littles are the submissive or bottom in both relationships and scenes to adults and caregivers. Utilizing ageplay roles enhances the level of dominance or submission in many situations. Since people naturally have a built-in response to a mother, father, or other caregiving figure, this type of relationship sometimes makes it easier for people to be either dominant or submissive.

Besides the given authority of family members, adults may try to trick, manipulate, or coerce littles into giving up something for them. Children are usually deferential to either strangers or professionals that they encounter, since parents have generally taught them to be polite. These adults may use their positions of power and authority to violate the little. News report are full of doctors, priests, teachers and other professionals that abuse their professional authority and exert power and control over their victims.

Society and societal roles often cast children into a role of dependency. Children are expected to respect the judgments of adults and conform to their preferences. They are also often not able to access many social and legal institutions, but must instead rely upon adults to access them on their behalf. Caring or being responsible for children also provides a sense of power or control to the caregiver (Kinkaid, 1992). In essence, children are not in control of their own lives.

Littles also have a desire not to be in control. As adults, many times we wish to regress, to not deal with our adult feelings and to be able to act and react childishly. Having someone to take care of our needs, deal with our worries, take care of our responsibilities, and care for us is both relaxing and freeing (Greene, 2001). As adults, we tend to look more sentimentally upon the powerlessness and dependency of childhood.

Littles in Control

> *Nikki's Daddy was done. He had already been dragged around the amusement park, taken her on rides, pushed her on the swing sets, bought her snacks and souvenirs. Towards the end of the day, he finally put his foot down. "Nikki, you just don't need any more stuffed animals. I've already bought you two today!" Nikki's deep brown eyes stared at her father, then widened, and tears started to run down her cheeks. Her mouth opened and a great wail came out between sobs. Her father looked nervous and worried as the crowd stared at him, expecting him to do something. "Honey?" he said hesitantly, stepping towards her. This only increased her bawling as she threw herself on the ground. People stopped and stared, watching what would happen. He knelt down next to her. "Um, it's ok baby, we'll get you that stuffie." Miraculously, the tears dried up and she stood up with an excited look on her face, taking off running towards the shop.*

Not all children are subordinate to adults. Some children are stubborn, stuck-up or bratty. On the other hand, some adults are whipped, have a desire to please their children, or are intimidated by their children and give into their wants. Veruca Salt from the *Willy Wonka* movies and book is an excellent example of a little as a dominant figure. She bullies her father into giving her exactly what she wants and complying with her demands. In this case, the little is trying to manipulate the adult into doing something that benefits them. The little is in control and the initiator of actions in this scene. With a Veruca Salt type of scenario, the father is trying to avoid negative stimuli, such as Veruca throwing a temper tantrum or acting out through complying with her wishes.

- Especially how I'm treated (and how I can make a fuss and act like a brat) is one of the things I enjoy most in little mode.

Some children are also very in touch, in control, and open with their sexuality. Although not clear about the consequences, children are often curious and excited about their sexuality. A performance piece by Barbara DeGenevieve is an excellent example of the sexual agency or desires of children and the power that they can have over sexual encounters with adults (DeGenevieve). In the performance piece, a female child enjoys the sensation of sexual play, as well as having a curiosity about sexual acts. Especially in this culture today, which has such concerns with pedophilia and child molestation, many don't consider or want to believe the fact that children could encourage or initiate sexual interactions.

Insisting that a little girl is a princess and should be treated like royalty is an example of where a little would wield control over bigs. In this example royalty, being in a legitimate position of power over others, would be the justification for children to wield power and authority, even over adults. The indulgent princess could order courtiers or citizens to perform any sort of action that she desired, all with the power of the crown behind her.

Likewise, a student who is trying to seduce a teacher or offering favors for a better grade would be another example of littles taking action and controlling a situation with bigs. In this scenario, the student is offering the teacher pleasure in return for other considerations. The little offering something that the big desires can be a good goal of a scene.

Littles have some tricks and techniques that they can use to acquire power and control bigs. Littles have the option to accuse bigs of misconduct, threaten them with exposure, or blackmail them (Kinkaid, 1992). Littles are also able to emphasize their own natural charm, weakness, helplessness, or vulnerability to manipulate caregivers into providing for them, getting what they want, or protecting them. They are also able to use their own innocence, sexuality, naughtiness, and the fact that they are young as excuses for their own behavior. A little could use their innocent face and pathetic voice to cover up for their cruel actions or dark acts (Greene, 2001).

Currently, the changing boundaries of what is acceptable for children can be pushed as another method of manipulation. Children can do this by informing bigs that things are different now than when they were children. In addition, littles can push bigs with more permissive parenting styles even further through clever manipulation.

There are several methods that allow littles to get the upper hand. One way is by having parents act more as friends than guardians. Many bigs want to remember their own past, and tend to indulge children, as that is what they would have wanted to happen to them.

Switching Dominance Roles

- I'm a little, but I'm also a switch. I get into the headspace through the dynamics of power struggles.

Many ageplay scenes are perfectly designed for switches. A fluid power dynamic within a scene would make it unpredictable, interesting, would increase the excitement, and provide a wider array of possibilities for the scene to explore. For example, one partner could start in control, have that control wrested away by the other partner, and then finally it could get taken back by them. For example:

> *Violet and Heather Anne were sisters who got along fine, most of the time. Heather Anne was a bully and a brat, however, and often pushed around her younger sister. After hiding her stuffed unicorn for the umpteenth million time and bullying her around for the morning, Violet got upset. Although younger, Violet was definitely the stronger of the two, Heather Anne being a delicate little flower. Violet yanked Heather Anne's head and pushed her down over the bed, then flipped up her skirt and started to paddle her. Heather Anne went from shrill mocking to sobbing and pleading quickly.*

Some ageplay couples focus mainly on each other and eschew playing with other individuals. These types of couples often seek out others for socialization but not play. If both people in these types of couple enjoy being diapered, the partners would need to function essentially as switches and alternately act as the caregiver; for example, diapering each other as needed.

This sort of scenario could also occur when littles get together but lack a dedicated caregiver. In this instance, the person who is playing the older or more outgoing child may attempt to bully the younger child.

Now that we've spoken about who takes control, we'll talk a little more about caregivers, including what they do, how they interact with littles, and the styles that they use.

Caregiving Styles & Tasks

One could use three basic types of caregiving or parenting styles with ageplay (Phelan). These parenting styles describe the manner in which children and adults interact. Parents use these same parenting styles with actual children. Each style is different and will result in different behaviors from children, as well as different dynamics between child and adult.

Authoritarian

Bernice was upset. Linda, her daughter, had quite a messy room. Bernice stood with her one hand on her hips and the other forced out, finger waggling in her daughter's face. "Linda, you are my daughter and this is unacceptable!" The little girl bit her lip and looked away. "You will clean up this room. Now! I will be back to check on you in an hour. In addition, I am grounding

you for three days. Let's not make it be any longer."
Linda sniffled and got to work.

The authoritarian parenting style is typically what one thinks of when they think of overbearing parents or controlled children. With this style, parents are clearly in control of their children and act sternly and unsympathetically. This parenting style is good for children who like punishment and strict, rigid guidelines.

Permissive

Bernice was upset. Linda, her daughter, had quite a messy room. Throwing up her hands, she cried out, "Linda, this is enough! C'mon let's clean it up, sweetie! When we get it all clean, I'll take you out for ice cream!" Linda smiled and started to throw things in her closet.

A permissive parenting style would mean that the parent attempts to befriend the child and really shows little control over the child at all. Children with permissive parents have much more freedom than children of other parenting styles. Bigs that use this sort of style would be excellent as being the bottoms or submissives in ageplay relationships. They would simply tolerate their child's behavior, maybe complain, but not actually command the child. When they wanted compliance, they would bribe or cajole the child.

Authoritative

Bernice was upset. Linda, her daughter, had quite a messy room. She shot her a stern look. "Linda, you know that we need our rooms and the house clean so we can get around easily and find things." Linda blushed a bit and looked down at her feet. "It appears to me

*that you haven't done a great job at keeping your room
clean. Spend some time cleaning it up, or else you can
go without your computer for the week."*

Authoritative parents allow children to be active in the growing process
by giving them options, choices, and help in setting the rules that they need to
obey. These choices allow the child to become more responsible for their actions
and behavior as well as learning about consequences. This parenting style seems
to be the best fit with long term or 24/7 ageplay relationships. This parenting style
could take the place of negotiation in the scene, by giving the child a limited set of
choices that they can follow. Punishment is also easy within this parenting model,
as the parent can offer a choice between doing something responsible (like chores)
or getting a punishment (such as a spanking).

For example, Mauricio spoke about his parenting style, which is most
closely identified as authoritative, when ageplaying:

*One of the challenges that I have encountered is knowing
how much authority to utilize. For me, it is hard to
determine how much structure and authority I should be
using at a certain time. Kids will be kids, so they deserve
to play and create some chaos. Finding the right time to
step in is sometimes difficult. I tend to issue a couple of
warnings and then head to discipline. I know that some
people need a stricter regimen and others prefer things
more lax. I might change; I guess I will have to see how
things go.*

Tasks of Caregivers

- I am always the adult in my ageplay. I am very eclectic, and will try to find a good balance with the needs of my partner, and that connection always has to come first – like most play, it's best if all parties walk away enjoying themselves. I especially enjoy being nurturing (feeding, bathing, cuddling, story time, singing songs, etc.). For masochistic or naughty littles I can also enjoy discipline from mild to hard, but even there I like to come back to nurturing in the end.

This section illustrates some of the tasks that caregivers perform for or with littles. Many caregivers go beyond these blanket categories in their relationships. The consistency of these interactions builds trust between partners.

Caregiving

Relationships are built upon an accumulation of small tasks and interactions. Bonds between littles and caregivers can be stimulated and encouraged through traditional bonding activities, such as feeding and affection. The concrete tasks of caregiving are also very important and a vital part of the exchange between the caregiver and the little.

Supporting

Many bigs that are caregivers also provide emotional or moral support. This support could manifest itself in several different ways. Depending on the dynamics of your relationship, this support could be deep and profound. Bigs can offer praise for good behavior or positive actions. Bigs also provide encouragement to littles to be responsible or perform certain actions. Guidance is another form of mental support that bigs can provide.

Scolding

Bigs often need to vocalize displeasure with their littles in order to get them to comply with demands or to demonstrate that something that they did was wrong. Sometimes these vocalizations should be loud, in order to impress the importance of the message, while other times (especially when in public), there can be softly whispered stern threats and reminders.

Drawing Limits

One of the tasks of bigs is drawing limits and setting boundaries. It is a fine line. On one side, bigs need to let littles be littles, let them have fun and enjoy their headspace. On the other hand, littles need to adhere to the rules, wishes, and desires of their bigs. Bigs should not be hesitant to enforce rules, guidelines, and limits. Many littles thrive knowing that there are guidelines and limits to their lives and behaviors. Punishment can be necessary and demonstrate that there are consequences to poor choices or inactivity.

Setting up or Controlling Scenes

Although many scenes are dynamic and a product of the partners, bigs can control and guide the scene in several different ways. Oftentimes, this can be through verbalizations, actions, and the pacing of the scene. Some ways that littles can control a scene include egging on a partner, misbehaving in order to provoke a reaction or bratting. It is important to remember that as a caregiver, you are generally in control of the scene (unless negotiated differently), so do not be afraid to use the power and authority that you are given. If your partner is acting up, then they desire a stricter reaction from you.

Now that we have looked at some of the different tasks that caregivers do during ageplay scenes, we will examine some of the different emotions that can be present. These emotions can vary widely and can be one of the main reasons that people ageplay.

Emotions in Ageplay Relationships

- There is also a difference, to me, between emotional codependency and emotional support. I don't expect someone to constantly think of my needs first and foremost, nor do I expect them to drop everything for me as everyone has their own lives and needs. However, I do wish to be thought of and considered, and for my love and respect to be reciprocated. Being a little requires one to be strong, and it takes a special Daddy or Mummy to recognize and work with that strength.

Due to the child-like wonder, desire, and disposition of the little, emotions in ageplay relationships are exaggerated and felt more deeply. This in turn sparks a more robust emotional reaction from bigs. In addition, thinking of childhood stirs up powerful memories and emotions (Greene, 2001). This amplification of emotion is often desirable and is one of the attractions of ageplay for many individuals.

Ageplay scenes express a wide range of emotions and desires. There seems to be tendency for many ageplayers (but not all) to conform to societal stereotypes. For example, many girls want to act like good little girls, while many boys prefer to be naughty, mischievous boys.

Positive emotions seem to be the most common in many ageplay scenes. Like many kinky activities, the unconditional positive emotions that are conveyed in some ageplay scenes are not generally found in everyday life. Reassurance, love, and affection all feel good to receive and harken back to childhood, when these emotions were simple. Giving positive emotions is also mentally rewarding as well, as you are making the other individual feel positive, and can see their reaction; often those feelings get reciprocated.

For example, reaffirming and telling someone that they are a "good girl" or "good boy" makes many people feel warmly, especially those who get only a small amount of praise otherwise. This phrase reinforces the good feelings with approving words, as well as reassuring actions, like a pat on the head or stroking. In fact, there are 178 fetishes relating to being a "good girl" on Fetlife, and 46 relating to being a "good boy" (Fetlife, 2011). This type of praise brings up many positive associations and remind people of good experiences or achievements from childhood.

Sometimes in ageplay scenes, and infrequently in relationships, play can focus on negative emotions. The negatives emotions are often desired in order to attain catharsis, cleansing, or for people to travel to a difference mindset (such as different varieties of subspace). These negative emotions can manifest in a variety of different ways.

For feelings like shame and guilt, for example, some people use scenes as a method of being held accountable for things that they feel they need to improve upon in everyday life. Spanking or having other punishments for being late, neglecting errands or tasks, and/or for overspending are common. The idea of punishment and redemption form the basis of some of these scenes. For example, after the spanking, the infraction is cleared and positive feelings resume.

> *For me, it is a chance to be vulnerable. It is a time when I do not have to have it all together, I can be taken care of and feel innocent.*

Jealousy and betrayal, or other negative emotions, can manifest through different types of scenes. These other negative emotions are more due a desire to experience the emotions instead of the aftereffects. Through role-play, you can safely experience negative emotions in a controlled state, without having to deal with any sort of fallout or repercussions for the actions.

Mentioning love also tends to be something that happens more quickly in ageplay scenes than in other kinds of scenes. At many times, the mention of love begins as part of a scene, as many scenes that involve positive emotions and reassurance between bigs and littles incorporate statements of love and affection. This is especially true in relationships where love is typical, such as those between a parent and a child. The statement of love in a scene may not reflect love outside of the roles and should not be confused as such. Unconditional love is a part of an idealized childhood however, and those sentiments often get conveyed through play. Even the play of unconditional love, which is the rarest kind of love, the kind for which we all search and strive, can be emotionally satisfying (Greene, 2001).

Sexual and Nonsexual Ageplay

This section will look into some of the dynamics, circumstances, and activities throughout this continuum.

Nonsexual Ageplay

Jeffery loved waterslides. There was nothing like crashing down the tubes, spinning around, splashing down, getting soaked, and then running back to the top of the slide to do it over again.

The childlike innocence and fun is rewarding for those that choose to engage in nonsexual ageplay.

Those that enjoy nonsexual ageplay revel in the fun and games, emotions, and good times of simply playing and acting young. This could include playing with a range of toys, child-like games, video games, cartoons, crafts, or coloring. This could also include outings to toy stores, play grounds, or out to the movies.

Cuddling

> *Leslie and Michelle were both between partners. They felt alone and needed some reassurance. Neither one can remember which one suggested it first, but soon they saw each other almost nightly and started to cuddle each other. Just the warmth of another body next to yours, warm, reassuring arms around you, and the feeling of another person who wants you near and cares for you, was enough for them.*

Cuddling can be sexually intimate for some, but it is mostly non-sexual, and used for reassuring and comforting. Hugs, slaps on the back, and reassuring arms over shoulders also are other methods for comfort and reassurance. The intimacy and physical closeness allows people to be close and nonsexual at the same time. It is also a way to express emotions or show sympathy. For example:

- But for me it was the intimate love (snuggling, cuddling) especially when I was diapered for bed, where I felt there was an inner child that craved the nurturing and intimate aspects of the relationship.

Sexual Ageplay

- Be yourself. I am a sexual ageplayer. I enjoy sex while in little headspace. Being guided, directed, taught and even "taken advantage of" from time to time are very arousing to me, and that is perfectly fine as I have no sexual interest in children and do not condone anyone else doing so. But I've discovered that it only hurts me if I try to deny this part of myself, and I am a much happier partner and mother when I'm able to be myself and not put up a false front of what I'm "supposed" to be.

Those that enjoy sexual types of ageplay may also enjoy the nonsexual ageplay activities but incorporate sexual elements into their play styles. This can include things like "playing doctor," body exploration, and sexual encounters with other littles or bigs. Once again, the power disparity, taboo nature, and the portrayal of innocence are factors in what makes this type of play intriguing to people. In this section, we will examine some of the different possibilities for sexual ageplay.

Kissing

> *Every time that I went over to Wendy's house, I was sure to dress up. I had a major crush on Wendy's father and simply couldn't help myself. Fortunately, Wendy was oblivious or else I would have been so embarrassed. My insides clenched whenever both of us were in the house. I would look for -any- excuse to talk to him. It finally got to the point where I could not help myself anymore. I needed him. While Wendy was on the phone, I decided to make my move. With palms sweating, I finally snuck down the hall to their room, took a quick breath to steady myself and turned the knob. I nearly squealed when I saw him shirtless on the bed napping. Shutting the door silently behind me, I took the steps to the bed quickly and quietly. Not wanting to disturb him, I perched next to the bed and took a closer look at him, drinking him in with my eyes. Finally, I closed my eyes, bent down and my lips met his. I could feel the passion pouring between us. His eyes fluttered awake and he gasped, "Rylee!"*

Kissing is sometimes a simple thing that people overlook and take for granted once relationships progress beyond a certain level. From an innocent kiss, to reflecting a caring interaction, to sexual passion, kisses can reflect many different emotions. Since it is so versatile, kissing is also an action that can switch, flip, or be twisted. A scene could start with some innocent kissing and move towards more passionate kissing as a gateway to other sexual activity.

Masturbation

> *Ever since she started feeling these urges and discovered how to satisfy them she became a collector. Jamie was always on the lookout for something new to play with. Underneath her bed was littered with thick candles, over-sized pencils, and markers. Rarely was there a night that she didn't fall asleep with part of her collection inside of her. She was playing with herself and drifting asleep when there was a rap on the door. She paused for a moment, "Yeah?" Her father opened the door and stepped into the room. He paused and sniffed a little bit, scrunching up his face. Then he bent down, kissed his little girl, and wished her goodnight. As soon as he closed the door, a look of embarrassment crossed her face, but she started back up furiously.*

Masturbation is generally one of the first sexual experiences that individuals encounter. Because of this, that topic is usually filled with emotion. Whether we feel pleasure or confusion, the budding of sexuality is an exciting time. Becoming sexual is often seen as the end of childhood and the beginning of adulthood (Postman, 1982).

The time of budding sexuality sometimes fills people with uncertainty, as one is exploring and building their sexual identity. People often have to hide their masturbation from other family members. The secrecy and shame of being discovered masturbating could also be fodder for scenes.

Oral Sex

Andy and Michael had been best friends for a long time. They were together all of the time and found themselves in all sorts of trouble. Now that they were entering adolescence, they had started to feel all sorts of feelings and emotions. After having stolen some porno mags from the Quick-Mart, they were certainly curious. They were both very horny and needed some release. Neither of them wanted to go first, so they both agreed to go at the same time. They stripped off of their clothes and their excitement became apparent. They laid down head-to-foot, counted down and after the count of one both lowered their heads onto each other's rigid penises. They both moaned and sucked, loving the sensations and slowly losing their concerns. Picking up their pace, both of them moved closer and closer to cumming in each other's mouths.

Oftentimes, kissing can lead to oral sex. Oral sex is often seen as more innocent, less threatening, or less dangerous than other forms of sex. It's often the first form of sex that people experience, thus it should figure prominently into scenes. It seems more like an introductory experience.

Anal Stimulation

Benjamin had not been pooing rightly lately. The laxatives hadn't been even been working. His mommy, Jenny, put on a rubber glove and smeared a couple of fingers with petroleum jelly. She had already taken off his diaper, so with her ungloved hand, she spread his butt cheeks and could feel him tense up. She eased one finger at first gently into his anus. As the finger entered him, Benjamin's tenseness slowly eased out of him and

*as she pushed into him up to her knuckle, Jenny could
hear Benjamin moaning a little bit. She reached around
and could feel his tiny turgid member. "There, there,
Benji," she cooed, as she started to stroke him.*

Anal activities are the focus with many diaper lovers. Anal stimulation
could also figure in prominently with some scenes. Whether it is simply a finger
stimulating the inside or outside of the anus or anal sex, anal stimulation can be
pleasurable for both partners. For some scenes, anal stimulation may also be a
substitute for penile/vaginal sex in teens.

Sexual Intercourse

*Even though she felt confused, Katie had needed this
so much. She was lying with her back pressed against
the bed and her legs in the air. With his hands between
her thighs, her Daddy pushed her legs apart to reveal
her smooth sex. She looked away with embarrassment
thinking that he could both see and smell her arousal.
He took the slight girl in his arms and slowly pushed his
turgid member toward her, the head wedging between
the slightly parted lips of her pussy. She gasped. Her
mind raced and screamed, the dual thoughts of, "This is
so wrong," and "God, this feels great," all at the same
time. Encouraged, Daddy pushed his naked cock further
into his daughter's virgin hole. It was a tight fit, but her
pussy was eager to take the hard shaft further into it and
was weeping with her juices at the thought. "Daddy's
going to fuck his little girl good tonight, isn't he?" "Oh,
yes Daddy!" She moaned as the shaft sunk deeper and
deeper into her. She felt like she was on fire, consumed
with lust and passion. Eventually, Daddy had filled her
up with his cock and was pressed tightly against her.
She felt divine and so little underneath the strong, big
man. She started to get into a rhythm, pistoning his cock*

and out of her, the length of the shaft alternately filling her up and being prepared to be thrust back into her. She could not stop the thoughts of her times with her Daddy and that she came out of the very same penis that was inside her right now. She was lost in her head and overcome by the pleasure of being with Daddy. Time passed but it was simply a blur to Katie. Daddy sped up his thrusts and started to tense. To be receptive for her Daddy, Katie tried to spread her legs open a bit more. With grunts, twitches, and moans on both of their parts, a torrent of cum released and they both clung to each other.

Many people have strong thoughts and emotions surrounding sex, thus it's not surprising that intercourse also plays a large role in many scenes. Whether it's losing your virginity, taking a new boyfriend or girlfriend, being found out or discovering your sexuality, intercourse can be the goal of a scene or simply a side effect of other aspects of the scene.

- I am a sexual ageplayer looking for a partner. It's an amazing world and you can delve into many different subcategories of ageplay. One fantasy I have would be an agreed upon "abusive guardian" scenario including some light bondage, spankings and punishments for no reason, and being turned into "mommy's sex slave" but still being naive to what was happening (or at least pretending to be naive).

Scenes can depict many different types of sexual intercourse. For example, one type of scene could focus on one partner trying to talk the other partner into sex, while the other partner resists. This scene could either entail verbal or physical coercing. Another example is the consummation of puppy love or a loving relationship.

Sexual activity also is a cause or a forum for expressing different emotions. Some positive emotions could be excitement and desire. Other, less positive emotions are vulnerability, anxiety, and guilt. Sexuality also displays a wide variety of different sensations. People can obtain pleasure from numerous different sources or acts. Learning about these new sources of methods of pleasure could be a fun instructional scene. Some littles could learn to enjoy "riding the horsey" or whatever other sexual games that are taught to them.

Training or Shaping Expectations

> *Kathy was the sexually experienced one and she had finally agreed to let Richard become her boyfriend. He was a quiet boy that kept following her around at school that had finally worked up the nerve to ask her out. They dated for a while. Richard was from a rich family. She liked that he had gave her several gifts. They had only done a little bit of kissing beforehand, but Kathy had waited long enough. "Richard, I'm going to show you what it's like to be a man and please a woman."*

Some sexual ageplay works on shaping sexual expectations or training partners to act in a certain way. Parents especially shape many things in their children's lives. This includes anything from teaching about things like Santa Clause, to sharing expectations and modeling behaviors like being a good partner. Since our sexuality is shaped in many ways in our early years, it makes sense that teaching, learning, and shaping would be part of sexual scenes. Partners also shape our sexual expectations about how we and/or others are supposed to act in a sexual arena.

This type of play could be used to teach someone how to behave sexually by pleasing the other person first, what one should expect from a sexual encounter, what are normal sexual practices, what are normal sexual roles, and how to interact with others. For example, a "bad girl" could be taught that they are just good for practicing sex and should be receptive to all sexual offers.

Secret Trysts or Betrayals

Megan was saving herself for her true love. She had to sneak out, but she had just told her mom that she was going to spend the night with Molly. Her mother would never know. Finally! She had taken a cab to the hotel with some money that he had sent her. He had left the hotel door propped open, and as she entered, she could hear the shower going. The outside door closed with a loud click. Her rain-covered outer coat softly crumpled as it hit the floor. Her heels made a soft clacking sound on the tiled part of the floor as she moved past the bathroom and over to the mirror. She wanted things to be perfect for their first time. Standing in front of the mirror, she adjusted her hair and then smoothed down the silky lingerie that he had sent her to wear for tonight. She checked that her tiny bosom was accentuated and made sure that her lipstick was perfect. He had instructed her to shave, and she was bare all over. She heard the shower turn off and she felt herself growing wet with anticipation. She crawled onto the bed, posing herself seductively, and made sure that her long blonde hair was flowing and lying teasing across her breasts. He stepped out of the bathroom in just a towel, saw her crumpled coat, and gazed towards the bed. His face erupted in a smile, his full beard pulled up by his mouth. "Baby!" His voice was thick with anticipation and she smiled as she noticed that he was becoming aroused at the sight of her. "Oh, Daddy," she said. "It's been so long since I've seen you!" she cried out as she spread her legs for him. Her parents had been divorced for a couple of years now and the courts did not allow her father to visit her. The towel dropped as he quickly moved to embrace his daughter.

Part of the allure of some sexual acts at an earlier age is the taboo nature of the act. Whether you role-play sneaking around, avoiding parents, or finding places to make out, these are all part of raising the level of excitement in the scene. Whether just sneaking around out of the sight of your parents, cheating behind your partner's back, or cuckolding your significant other, adding deception to a scene can be quite easy. Once again, it is the energy of secrets and allure of the forbidden that give these scenes extra energy (Greene, 2001).

Pregnancy/Impregnation

> *It was just a couple weeks after Brooke's birthday. She had noticed that it had been a while since her last period but was not sure how long. Here she sat in her friend's bathroom, pants down, having just peed on the pregnancy test kit that she had just shoplifted from CVS. As the time ticked by, she ran through the list of her boyfriends from the last couple of months. None of them had really stayed around that long, at least not once they had got into her panties. After the time elapsed, she looked down and started to cry. Emblazoned on the tester; the big red "X" showed she was certainly pregnant. However, who was the father?*

Many teens have been worried or concerned about pregnancy during childhood. Due to it being such an emotional issue, there is bound to be play surrounding this topic. Playing off that fear, and purposely being impregnated or threatened to be "just a baby machine," could also be an effective scene. There are also the feelings of confusion about what to do, how to proceed, and how your life will change.

Becoming or being pregnant, especially as someone who cannot support themselves and/or a child, is a situation of extreme dependency. The ties of conceiving a child bind people together and enhance dependency. There is also the interplay of societal and parental reactions, as well as repercussions to the pregnancy.

Now that we have spoken about some of the different activities that can occur during ageplay, we will discuss how some of these activities make people feel. These feelings or headspace can be quite pleasurable. The next section will discuss this phenomenon in more detail.

How to Get into your
Headspace and Back Out

Sometimes the littlest things set Charlie off. Going to the mall was the most distracting. Everything was so tempting and drew him in: the bright colors, children's clothes, and the toy stores. Those were especially bad. All he had to do was go in, find a gift from his wife, and then back out. But that KB Toys was such a draw...

Getting into a headspace or pleasurable mental state where you feel that you are in your role is often the goal of many scenes. Different physical triggers or mental routines help people initiate or get deeper into headspace, or more into character. Here are some comments that demonstrate the varied nature of headspace for littles:

- I usually get into the headspace of a little when I am feeling insecure. When I need to feel protected and like someone else knows better and is looking out for me. It feels like freedom. It feels like simple peace. Like a set of crayons has all the answers and nothing has to be complicated. I feel like I am truly loved.

- It is easy for me to get into my littles headspace because I love to be a little girl and NOT have responsibility.

- My little headspace is filled with shame, arousal, and excitement.

- Little space kind of feels like being drunk, but without the loss of any inhibitions or control, you just feel free to be whomever you want. You find small things fascinating and exciting. I'm much more emotional as a little more affectionate and needy.

This section will examine some of the different areas that people find helpful to bring about or enhance their headspace. In reality, a combination of these factors is the most likely to induce headspace.

Natural Reaction

For some people, transitioning into an ageplay headspace is natural and fluid. This could possibly place those individuals more on the literal side of the ageplay spectrum. They may also tend to think of themselves as needing a higher intensity of ageplay interactions as well. Many people spoke about how this happens naturally to them:

- The innate personality characteristics of a "little" provide cues that "press my buttons" innately. It is NOT something that I ever had to learn or practice.

- Use a specific memory trigger, like a toy or piece of music you remember.

  - Different triggers, just thinking about it, it's easy, like I'm 10.

  - It feels like a natural young child, my thinking is exactly the same. Sometimes I'm in and out of little space even in a session but that's only if I'm distracted by something.

- I wouldn't say it's hard, but it's hard to say how I get there. It's not like a switch gets flipped or something. Sometimes I see something, or something happens to me, or I just really need to destress. I do say that it takes a great deal of trust of the people that I'm with to go fully into headspace.

- For me, I can slip into it pretty easily, but I am always aware of the fact that if responsibility does call, I can slip back out on a second's notice. "Kita" does demand attention sometimes.

- As for how it feels it's more a different way of seeing things, feeling about things, responding to things etc. It feels less stressed, like I don't have demands on me that may or may not be able to be met because it just does not matter if the demands are there or if they can or will be met. I don't have a trigger, my little side is usually pretty much alongside my "big" side, just one steps forward as needed. I do tend to smile more when my little headspace is in front though.

- Wow...this is a difficult one, because for me it happens so naturally that I don't have to do any special thing to get into the headspace.

- I often go into little space if I'm excited or tired or if I have a whole weekend to myself. I don't ever DO anything to get there in purpose.

Getting into a Caregivers Headspace

- I am always a Daddy even in my "vanilla" life. I educate, guide, nurture, and exert some degree of control.

- Just naturally comes to me being a woman and wanting to be a mommy role. I just kinda do it.

In most cases, caregivers require very little time to transition into their headspaces. This may place caregivers more on the literal side of the ageplay spectrum as well. It may be easier for caregivers or bigs to live in their headspace, as the tasks that they engage in are similar to tasks that most adults perform. Their ordinary responsibilities of work, getting things done, and making sure that everything is in order are quite similar to those responsibilities that they take on during their caregiver role. If anything, being a caregiver adds some responsibilities and tasks to their repertoire.

Paraphernalia & Props

Some people go to one extreme, for example, building a nursery in their home, but even using simple objects can bring some ageplay scenes to life. These do not need to be overly complex or expensive. Things like a backpack, ruler, pencils, and textbooks are certainly enough to work with for a school or homework type scene. Some oversized items, like suckers, work well in order to have the little feel physically smaller. Having a few toys or crafts helps set the scene as well. Many people in the survey spoke about the items that they use when little:

- Usually rocking myself, or being rocked, baby talk, favorite pacifier, familiar song, it depends on what has been going on lately.

- I'm fairly new to the ageplay scene although I have done it all my life. I have had many series of blankets and I use them til are worn to shreds and keep buying more. My dad tried to take them from me as a five year old and that did NOT go well so he gave it back. So now here I am, a 23-year-old with two main blankies, and I'm sucking on a pacifier as I'm writing this.

- Little: children's movies and books, my stuffed animal, being around other littles, drinking from a sippy cup, wearing bright colored laces on my shoes/boots, etc. It's not difficult for me. Big: When my Daddy starts acting little and wants things that another little can't do easily, I just go into that mode automatically. Being around other brats normally puts me into big mode first, unless I know I can go into little mode (aka there's a Big around to watch the littles, so I don't have to).

- I view it as a slide...starting at the top, with all the "little" supplies...and as the diaper/clothing is put on, the lotions, the feeling of the nipple of a pacifier/bottle in my mouth, the texture/smell of a teddy bear snuggling close...by the time you reach the bottom of the slide (using all the paraphernalia for age play) you are regressed.

You can greatly add to the realism of a punishment scene using household implements for spanking, such as wooden spoons. Many people have a reaction to this and could possibly recall emotions or feelings from childhood. Other items that stimulate the senses, such as positively associated tactile sensations and different scents, can also work to engage people in headspace.

Clothing and Accessories

Using clothing is an excellent way to get deeper into a role-play. Just a different choice of outfits or styles of clothing can make you feel different and allow you to engage your role more fully. Remember, there is no "right" dress code for ageplay.

Some ribbons in your hair, a baseball hat, or a brightly colored print t-shirt may be all that you need. Other people go to further extremes, with frilly dresses, onsies, and diaper covers. There is no longer such a thing as clothes for children. High heels, bikinis, and other clothes that were traditionally for adults are now marketed towards children (Postman, 1982). You may want to emphasize your role by dressing in a typical manner. This could include cartoons on t-shirts, brightly colored clothing items or other typical clothing for children (like footie pajamas).

Many adults simply wear jeans, t-shirts, and tennis shoes. This type of wear was traditionally for children, before it transitioned over to mainstream culture (Postman, 1982). Once again, because of this, you may want to dress to emphasize an aspect of your role. For example, a bigs typical costume could include an apron for housewife mothers or a business suit for working fathers.

Here are some comments from ageplayers in regards to clothing:

- Costumes can add a lot of fun and depth to a scene. I have a whole other wardrobe developing for my character!

- Putting on a diaper and an onesie or footed sleeper helps to set the mood. For me, it's about total immersion. Wetting and messing my diaper, sleeping with my Pooh Bear, sucking on a pacifier or baby bottle filled with milk, makes it easy. Getting back to "big" for me is as simple as changing back into big boy underwear and clothes. My "little" head space lives for the moment and is care free. My "big" head space is left to handle all the worries of life.

- I love the feeling of my cares and worries tumbling from my shoulders when I'm in little space. I love the way ruffles and lace brush my skin. I love the give of my stuffies and sweet shelter of my blankie when I pull them close and I love that I finally have come to terms with this part of me and that it is okay to be a little.

- There are special items and rituals I save just for getting me into little headspace. Certain outfits or items of clothing, hair bows and barrettes, my mood, and even some of my perfumes are "little only" and only touched/worn when I'm feeling little or need to be little. I don't have much experience in an actual, clearly defined ageplay relationship yet so can't speak to that, but imagine that it would just be something I'd feel and follow when with my Mummy or Daddy.

- I guess that the one thing that helps me get into either big or little headspace is what clothing I'm wearing. Little clothes always signal little-space, while adult clothing or lingerie signals an adult space.

Thrift stores are often wonderful places to find clothing for ageplay. Although the clothes may not be perfect, the price is often right for things like suits, t-shirts with an ageplay theme (Best Daddy ever, or employee shirts from Day Care Centers), cartoonish print clothes and plaid skirts. Although they may need some tailoring, even with the costs of alternations, these pieces are often less expensive than other sources.

For some costumes, depending on the factors, you might be better off going to the source of official garments rather than buying fetish costumes. For clothing like school outfits and cheerleader costumes, you may be able to find something in your size for the same price or less than what a fetish costume would cost. Often these are higher quality pieces, which hold up to more use. There are some suggestions for these sorts of shops in the *Resources* section at the end of the book. Please remember that these are not kinky establishments, so do not be overt when dealing with them.

Many places online sell clothing especially for those into ageplay. There is a wide range of items available, from adult sized onsies to elaborate dresses and so forth. Many of these pieces are beautiful and custom made, but often they have a high price tag as well. However, for the perfect outfit, there may not be any other way to obtain it.

Online forums and groups often post finds that individuals have located in ordinary stores but could be used for ageplay. This may be something like adult sized footie pajamas at Target or other things along that line. Please remember that these are not kinky establishments and do not be too overt when dealing with them.

Accessories like pacifiers and hair ribbons can add to an outfit as well, or substitute for an outfit when one is not available. For girls, cheap jewelry and poorly applied makeup may be helpful in some scenes. For boys, headbands, bandannas, or things like pocketknives can serve as accessories.

Physical Changes and Positioning

Some people choose to alter their bodies slightly for ageplay. This could include shaving, as a lack of hair generally mean immaturity, removing piercings, and, for women, possibly flattening the breasts. People also change their hairstyles, mostly into more childish versions, such as pigtails and ponytails.

Physical positioning may also be important to some people. Ageplayers may want to be aware of their positioning and height. For example, adults may want to stand over littles, to give the perception of height. Littles may want to spend some time laying, crawling, or crouching in order to feel smaller during scenes. Lying down is a very helpless or passive position (Greene, 2001). This physical hierarchic demonstrates a nonverbal source of power.

Language and Speech

The language and tone that is being used when role-playing influences the scene to a large extent. The sweet tones of loving and affection, when contrasted to the stern yells of anger, really demonstrate an emotional breadth that can be utilized in different types of scenes. Volume is another important aspect in language. If someone is angry, you can be soft, low, and threatening, or yelling loudly to convey your emotions. Here are some examples of language and tone that came from the survey:

- When I'm called little girl, or sweetie, or baby, it makes me feel very little and girly.

- My behavior depends sometimes or by how my Daddy treats me and talks to me.

- Being called "Baby girl" normally starts it. I feel elated, energized, revived.

- Being called baby girl or princess and being bathed and put in jammies or put into a diaper instantly gets me into little space. Usually it's very easy to get me there if I trust you, I don't age play with just everyone. So far, I've only been little around one person physically; it was for a whole day and was a wonderful experience and one I would love to do again. I feel cuddly and silly and things like flopping in his lap feel "right." I tend to get less vocal too. Everything just seems brighter and bigger and more wonderful and less bogged down than when I'm in big mode.

- All it takes is some erotic talk and role-playing a bit to make me feel like I'm a helpless little baby......it's extremely easy

- I find it very easy to get into headspace with my Daddy. It is the way He talks to me that gets me there. 'Good girl'...'that's my little girl'... those words do it for me.

- I feel little the second I see Daddy, hear his voice, or talk to him online. I also feel little in stressful situations or when I'm upset. This head space feels comforting. It feels safe. It feels a bit needy.

Many littles choose to alter the way they speak when in their littles' persona. Some choose to use simpler words, talk more slowly, and use less slang or poor grammar. Others simply use gibberish or cooing, such as how babies would speak. Others speak normally. Using a mix of these techniques also is a viable option.

For bigs, their tone is often more strict and authoritarian, or sweeter and more loving, while in a scene than otherwise. Using pet names for the little and the big can increase a sense of familiarity between partners during a scene. Here are some sample pet names for littles, although many more exist:

Girls:	Female Caregivers:
pumpkin little one young lady muffin little girl cupcake sweet pea baby girl	Mamoo Mummy Mumsy Auntie
Boys:	**Male Caregivers:**
tiger buddie dearie little man babykins pooh Babyboo Bunny bunkie	Daddy Dadoo Poppy Pops Papoo Unkie

Some names that children use are negative and derogatory and can be very effective in the proper scene. Using slurs like sissy, wimp, and crybaby can evoke a sense of powerlessness or a lack of self-control, which is desired in some scenes. These words are generally very emotionally charged.

Other words, which are forbidden for children, can contain power as well. For example, calling another little a "slut" could be hurtful. Children often use words that they know are naughty, even without knowing the definition of the word. Children as young as age six use these types of words (Postman, 1982). Take caution not to slip back into using an ordinary alternative sexuality vocabulary, as some of these words may be hurtful in a little headspace.

Activities

- Sometimes if I haven't had baby time in too long I'll subconsciously start to suck my thumb.

- Do what makes you feel comfortable and small. If there's something you used to get flak for that adult shouldn't do (coloring, watching children's movies, eating certain foods, wearing certain clothes, going to a toy store, and touching/playing with everything), do it. It will probably help you loosen up with your little side.

- It's quite easy for me. I tend to go in and out of headspace sometimes. Sometimes what gets me into it is just a cartoon on TV or being alone with my teddies and coloring book.

- From doing something "normal" adding in the ageplay elements into it.

- All it takes for me is to be put in diapers. Once the diapers go on, then I'm there.

- I find that just doing simple things like cuddling, coloring in a coloring book, eating ice cream sundaes makes me feel little again. I find it difficult sometimes but mostly it just comes when I want.

- To get me into "littles space" I have a routine. I get home, get seated for dinner and am fed like a child. Or after dinner, going for a bath, getting naked and being washed. When the bath is done, I should be dressed appropriately. It's generally a smooth transition, rather than being on one side or the other only (i.e. instead of "on or off" like a regular switch it is like a dimmer switch where it transitions from off to completely on). Currently, I must transition to little space by myself due to not having partner.

- I can use a nap to get me back into big space. When I wake up, I'm back in big space headspace and can pretend that the previous time of "consciousness" was a dream of being a little again. I can also use a reversal of this technique with something normal, like a bath. I use it for transitioning back to big space (by explaining that I "accelerated my growth" back into my adult mindset).

Transitioning into littles space by plunging in and doing activities that littles would do is possible and popular. For example, watching cartoons, coloring, or doing other childish activities helps some people get into or deeper into their headspace. Sometimes being diapered is an excellent transformation activity or ritual as well.

Partner Reactions

- I find it difficult to enter that headspace without a willing partner to help me along. I do have an online mommy who helps me, and we did meet once.

- It's something that is just usually there, but a big can definitely bring it to the surface quickly.

- For me, in my kink life, I've always been very "switchy"...I tend to try to find good people, focus on how I can connect with them (things we have in common, play we both might enjoy, where someone's head is at the moment, etc.) in the moment and let my play evolve from that. I might plan an event ahead with someone...but it's always WITH someone. So for me getting into the space is easy, it's just a matter of working out what role my partner needs that I can feel comfortable filling, then jumping into the play. I also don't sweat things not going perfect, so for me I'm not feeling nervous if things don't go well etc. That said, as the big, my job is relatively easy. I'm not the one really putting myself in a vulnerable place, like the little is. So often, I find myself in my space and then trying to help my partner find their way into their space, so to speak.

- My now girlfriend helps by mommying me. It's the first time I have been babied while age playing. Getting into a little's headspace is interesting. For me, it's kind of like a dreamlike state, and it's very emotional.

- Headspace just happens for me; I become a little most after a very intense scene with a top. I regress, and then I come back as my body returns to "normal." I think it has something to do with the person I'm playing with and everything going on around me.

- I get into little headspace when I have a loving partner who will help me age regress using diapers, bottles, cuddling, etc. It is not difficult to regress in that situation. It feels comfortable, relaxed, affectionate, and fun.

- For me it's easy but I have had a lot of practice in training when it is ok and when it isn't. I can easily jump into headspace by the way I'm treated combined with being diapered and in baby clothes, having child cartoons or music on, and having my paci, bottle, and/or teddy bear. I think I created headspace attachments to these things and with them it is ok to be in my little headspace.

- Usually a big will bring it out of me. Then there are just times with myself when it's more casual and fun, like coloring or dancing.

Sometimes having a partner and playing off their reactions enables people to get into headspace more quickly. Having a partner allows you to have someone to reflect and react to, can deepen your headspace by having to reply, or keeping you oriented to the scene. The partner connection is reinforcing, as it encourages you to push things or delve deeper into your role.

Environment or Surroundings

- Setup and environment is important. I find my best 'little space' occurs when I am alone and can control everything around me. TV shows, foods, music, clothes, and the room itself all works to awaken that mental state. It's not easy but when it works you know it. I knew I was in little space all the way when I was genuinely, not role-playing here, but truly afraid of the dark in a way I was not since I was a kid.

- All it really takes is for me to know that I'm in a safe environment and that nothing bad can happen. Little space feels relaxing and calm for the most part.

The environment and your surroundings are often important to entering into headspace. Children perceive the world with heightened senses and love to have their senses filled with delightful things. The atmosphere should reinforce a happy demeanor, be filled with bright colors, be warm and cheery, and allow playful activities (Greene, 2001). These spaces can be something as simple as a calm place with a couple of toys, to a dedicated nursery.

Balance

- I find I can't wear diapers on Sunday evenings because then I wake up small, and work is just too difficult in little space.

- It depends mainly what is required of me at the moment. If I do not have to do anything that's really "grown up" then I tend to slip into little headspace and tend to default there right now.

- I'm always in and out, at any given moment. Sometimes it is hard to stay in big space and vice versa.

- It is rather easy for me to regress in the right environment. I can also change back when necessary. I enjoy feeling dependent when I'm little and somewhat detached from thinking of any things of importance. It's somewhat like the feeling of relaxing on a beach in the Caribbean.

- It's difficult to me to have to put my "big girl" panties on.

- For me, my 10-year-old self is ALWAYS close to the surface, if not the dominant aspect of my personality. With my real life wife, there are times when she quite plainly tells me to grow up as she wants to be with the Big me, not the child.

- 90% of the time I find myself stuck at age 14 and sometimes even younger.

- I try to stay balanced between my adult and inner child sides. Both I feel are needed to be whole.

Having a balance and being in the appropriate headspace at the right time is quite important and a struggle for some. Interacting childishly in the wrong circumstances or with the wrong people could be awkward or embarrassing. One needs to leave headspace to take care of adult responsibilities, as well as to interact with friends and others.

Getting out of Headspace

- If I absolutely NEED to be big, it takes me a moment to clear my head and reorder things. A moment of silent meditation if you will. For my two-year-old headspace, I rarely just slip into it unless something triggers it, or my mommy or daddy call him out. It's a more thorough immersion and many adult-like thoughts are deeply buried. Coming out of that headspace takes a bit of effort and thought, and a need to do so as a catalyst.

Some people are able to integrate their role-play identity or child-like personality aspect very well with their everyday lives. One issue with those who primarily played little roles have had was limiting the amount of ageplay that they did. All the respondents to the survey acknowledged a need to come out of their headspace as a little and deal with adult issues in the real world. Some people had more difficulty with that task than others had and commented about this issue:

- That some want to throw the "adult" side away and be little 24/7.

- Not being able to get OUT of my little headspace and into my adult life.

Since it is difficult for some people to get out of their headspace, sometimes it is necessary for one to help people step out of their ageplay role or headspace. Here are some tips:

- Have them slowly count up from their ageplay age to their real age

- Have a transitional activity or possession that you can engage or use

- Speak the person's real full name sharply; this may snap them out of it

Emotional Reactions

Since everyone has had a childhood, and sometimes those that choose to engage in ageplay have less than desirable childhoods, people who ageplay need to be aware about negative emotions that may surface through play. Although many people have a good number of scenes with different partners and encounter no troubles or issues, there is a small chance that some sort of negatively impacting situation may arise.

Some ageplayers are concerned with dealing with abuse and other childhood trauma. People who have experienced negative episodes should direct their partners away from transactions, words, and physical actions that mimic those of their prior abuse. Some ageplayers with a history of negative episodes choose to engage in activities that mirror the negative episodes that they experienced as a method of working through these memories. Playing the scene has a significant difference, however. This time they are in control of what is happening. Ageplay is not a replacement for therapy and everyone in a scene such as just described should be aware of the past issues and possible emotional ramifications.

Negative emotional episodes are rarely kept in the unconscious or forgotten. However, memories could be buried or intentionally forgotten with cases of abuse (Van der Kolk & Fisler, R., 1995). It seems unlikely that an age player would run into a subconscious memory of these past incidents. Although unlikely, some of the other types of negative emotions or associations could surface. These sorts of memories or fragments of memories have been forgotten but not necessarily buried in the subconscious. A tone of voice, saying a particular phrase, or a certain action may be aroused by negative memories or fragments of memories. For instance, being hit or slapped in a certain manner may evoke a negative response from when the individual was in another emotionally charged situation in the past. The individual may not even remember the past incident, but simply feel a negative feeling or confusion.

When negative memories or associations arise, and the individual is in distress, it is best to end the scene. After all, you can always communicate and restart later on in a better headspace. Sometimes, initiating the type of aftercare that the individual enjoys may be helpful. The next section will address methods for recovery and transitions from scenes.

Aftercare, Drop & Caregiver Fatigue

- One challenge with ageplay is that I feel a little dirty afterwards, but with some talking and cuddling, that goes away.

Ageplay can be draining for both caregivers and littles. This drain becomes evident in several different ways. Either through running around or emotional excitement, littles often become tired. Caregivers become cranky when having to take too much control; the responsibility of caring for someone can take a toll as well. There are several different methods to alleviate and remedy these feelings. Everyone has individual and different desires and needs when it comes to aftercare. This section presents some suggestions.

Aftercare

- The one lingering memory I have so far is being cradled in a Dom's arms after a scene, snug under a blanket and with a bottle of water to sip. I was so contet I went for my thumb and he saw this and offered his own instead. He stroked my cheek and told me I was such a strong and good girl, and I knew right then that this was what I'd needed for so long without knowing it.

After doing a scene, some people need some time to be acclimated once again to the real world. Some people have rituals that they like to engage in that help them transition. Others are able to transition from a role instantly and almost seamlessly. This could also be a time for cuddling or for leaving the individual alone.

Just like any sort of scene, you should discuss and negotiate options and desires for aftercare. The need for aftercare may be more necessary in some age play scenes, especially those that involve punishment or some of the more negative emotions. You are responsible for your own transitions, as well as the ability to put yourself back together after a scene. Your partner can help you facilitate these actions, but in the end, you are responsible for yourself.

Drop

After experiencing time as a little, free of responsibilities, some littles experience a drop after the scene where the real world seems overly difficult or burdening. Thus, aftercare is especially important for these people, as is a gradual phasing back to the real age of the individual. This drop could feel depressing, you could have increased anxiety, or the world could seem overly dull. Some people may also feel somewhat disoriented when they drop their role and revert to their ordinary persona.

Transitions for some people are more involved than just receiving aftercare. Some more elaborate rituals can involve removing a symbolic piece of jewelry, changing out of their little's outfit and back into normal clothes, or slowly counting upward to their real age.

Caregiver Fatigue & Burnout

- Adult Babies require a lot of attention and energy and I am often drained dry after intensive play.

- Daddy wants to be daddy much less then I want to be little.

Caregivers are generally responsible for discipline, guidance, and setting limits. These can be stressful tasks and some caregivers can become burned out. This is especially true when they are already taxed by everyday life or extended scenes. To counter this burnout, some appropriate activities including cuddling, relaxing, and napping. Both caregivers and littles need to remember to take things in moderation, and reserve plenty of downtime for relaxing, cuddling and playing without pushing boundaries or acting up. Some possible solutions for minimizing burnout include:

- Take breaks from roles and scenes

- Allow the bottom or little to cater to the caregiver's needs

- Don't be afraid to make mistakes

- Communicate and talk about it

- Ask for understanding and help

- Don't be afraid to utilize corner time or time outs

- Set schedules for when to be in your roles or doing scenes

Next, we will look more into the experiences of several ageplayers and the different options for coming out or revealing your ageplay tendencies to other people.

Choosing About Coming Out with your Ageplay Roles

- I wish I could be more open about how much I love my partner, not just as himself, but as my brother. People are too quick to freak out, and I don't want people to treat us differently because they think we're pedophiles or something... which neither of us is in the least. Sigh!

Eventually, most people who are interested in ageplay, especially those that identify as littles, decide not to keep their fantasies and desires to themselves and open up to other people. Generally, this opening up or coming out first occurs online, where anonymity allows people to express themselves freely and specific forums and groups allow them to be open with people who have similar interests. This stage of coming out is helpful, as it reinforces that there are other people who share your interests, possibly understand your wants or desires, and who have gone through similar struggles. Oftentimes this leads to wanting to disclose to other individuals.

Overall, people who identify as bigs or caregivers generally do not feel as much need to disclose. This could be because they do not feel much different.

Society sees caregiver roles as traditional and socially desired. Another is that having someone dependent on you is a somewhat typical relationship dynamic.

Ageplayers often would like to explore their fetish with their partners. However, if the relationship does not primarily incorporate ageplay or other fetishes, there may be some tension in disclosing what turns you on to your partner. Sharing your fetishes with them requires a certain amount of trust. Since each relationship is different, the timing of the disclosure is something that has to be personal and occur when it feels right. Some people prefer to disclose earlier in a relationship, while others prefer to disclose later. Realize that after you disclose your fetish, it may be a deal breaker to some people. You should reassure your partner that your feelings and interests are not about something that they are lacking or something that they have done.

Tips for Coming Out

There are many factors to consider before deciding to either come out with your roles or not. If you do choose to come out to people, here are some helpful tips. These are basic tips for coming out; remember that you know your audience better than anyone else does and can tailor the message to them.

- Tell them what ageplay is at a very basic level. Describe your interests in a general fashion. You may need to tell them about what ageplay is not as well. See how they react to the news

- Give them time to integrate the information; don't bombard them with too much information or too many details at first

- Focus on "I" statements (i.e. "I feel that this is part of my life.")

- Reinforce that this is something that you want/initiated

- Explain that this is a tender, loving, caring relationship
Here is some advice direct from other ageplayers:

- I would only tell people who are trustworthy and open minded – not someone who will judge you outright. Some people need to know the difference between ageplay and pedophilia.

- When coming out to a sig other or potential play partner, roll it out like a Christmas present, not a disease.

- I have told a few close of friends about how W/we play. I explain it in a role playing way, which is really how W/we do play. They kinda laugh and say it must be fun, but I know they do not understand.

- The people that matter won't care ... and well do you really care about telling people that don't matter to you?

- I think you should only come out to a partner. My tip would be to introduce them to it slowly, not spring it all at once. Or, if ageplay is a large, defining aspect of your life, wear it on your sleeve, so to speak. And attract partners with similar interests.

- One person in my "vanilla" life knows and she thinks its fun, although I have not told her about the sexual parts of the ageplay that I engage in.

- I have always taken a slow approach, letting the other person develop a level of comfort, before I reveal more about the subject.

- Just because I told many people doesn't mean I can just get all dressed up and be little around them. That would be overwhelming and a breach of personal space. That doesn't mean someone won't be willing to try it with you. If they are then work on things gradually.

- My best friend knows. We started writing a sex blog together for fun. I wrote about what I was learning about BDSM and eventually admitted it was an interest of mine. She was (and still is) wary. I think the most important thing for me to tell people is that (in my mind) it has nothing to do with pedophilia (which is the conclusion I think many people immediately draw).

Most people only choose to come out to a certain category of individuals. We'll now look at some people's experiences and thoughts regarding coming out to different groups of people.

Out to Mostly Everyone

- I have a little rainbow letter-block bracelet I made that says <3Daddy's Boy<3 on it. That accidentally breaks the ice in most situations. Besides that, as they get to know me they simply know. I call my husband Daddy constantly, and he and I openly talk about things having to do with age play (and he tends to bring sippy cups to work).

- Everyone in my life except work and family know.

- Lifestyle friends, family, my Dadda and Momma... my bratty sister, um... long list.

   Some people are very casual about their ageplay desires and identity. Some people see this aspect as congruent with their personalities. The extent to which people may disclose will vary with their comfort level. More people are fine sharing general aspects and less comfortable with fine details. Some of the time, these behaviors could be classified as eccentricity or personality quirks.

Only to those in the Alternative Lifestyles

- I've only talked to like minded individuals about ageplay.

- At first, I thought there was something wrong with me so I felt really ashamed. But I just couldn't shake the feeling of rightness I had during our talks, so I started to do some exploring on the net and in my local kink group.

- It just happened that a friend of mine was struggling with a fetish that is even less understood than my own, so by helping and supporting him with links, talking on the phone, and trying to be a good friend while understanding his inner conflicts, I ended up helping myself, too.

- I am a sexual little. Putting on frilly socks and putting my hair in pigtails is arousing to me. Being in little space during sex is very fulfilling for me. Being aware of all this and finding communities where I'm definitely not alone has been a tremendous help. I wear my Mary Jane shoe pendant with pride and as a reminder that though I might be balancing the budget or doing laundry, my little is never far away.

- I am out in my local kinky scene, Leather and BDSM people, and to a few close vanilla friends. Some kinky people mock it, some are intrigued. It is hard to be a Leather baby.

- Yeppers, my wife, play partners, others in the kink community. In the kink community, I've just never felt the need to hide anything, I've always had such awesome support, and I haven't felt compelled to tell anyone not already knowledgeable about my kink play. That said, I have heard of others who have had much more negative experiences.

- Only to my friends in the lifestyle... We were talking about what we liked in the lifestyle and how we acted with our Dom's... It went well, they understood it.

Most people in the alternative sexuality community are likely to be accepting of your ageplay orientation. Many of those in The Scene have struggled with finding someone with whom to share their wants and desires. Even if they are different, they most likely will still understand basic concepts such as headspace, roles, and the fulfillment that you get from acting out your fantasies.

To Professionals

- I have an amazingly understanding and open-minded therapist who knows.

Some people choose to be open with professionals that they encounter. Some mental health professionals as well as some medical personnel may be able to have increased accuratcy treating conditions and ailments if they know some of your habits or outlooks. For example, if you are a heavy diaper wearer, that may be something that you might want to tell a health professional when dealing with a urinary tract issue.

To Your Partner, a Play Partner or Significant Other

> *"As for telling the boyfriend about it without sounding
> perverted: Sorry, can't help you there. It's going to sound
> perverted because the scenario you want to explore is
> all kinds of sick and wrong. Just own it when you tell
> him about it: "I know this is crazy and fucked up, but
> these stories really turn me on." You don't want to fuck
> kids; you want to pretend to be the kid your boyfriend
> fucks. He doesn't want to fuck kids; he wants to fuck you
> while you're pretending to be a kid." (Savage)*

Some ageplayers relate their examples of coming out to a partner:

- I'm just honest. I tell the story of my first age-play partner coming out to me. So far, it has been well received by the two subsequent lovers I shared it with. One wasn't interested in it. The other developed an interest for it, like I had. My tip: just be honest.

- Yeah, my girlfriend. We had been together a couple of months, and then found out she was already on Fetlife, and that we shared the same interests. It was literally like winning the lottery.

- I have opened myself up to a number of people over the years. The first, my (now ex) wife. Initially, she was taken aback. Sadly, I didn't say anything of my interests until four years or so into our relationship. She told me that "there is something wrong with you" and also said that as long as she didn't see/hear/know about it....she was ok with it. Years later, when we divorced, the point was made (after all was said and done) that my being a "baby" was a factor for the distance that she had from my physically/sexually. I have also established relationships with two people, where within the second or third dates, it became a topic. One was a very negative and sad experience. The second was a bit more accepting, and she had participated, by not only being my "mommy," but she would also want to wear diapers (while out shopping etc.) and we role-played a few times. I think she did it more to feel what I felt...

seeing/knowing the enjoyment I got out of it. She sadly has moved away...and I have not had a female ageplay partner since (3 years now).

- I have only come out to my husband. My husband and my Daddy are two different people. It was hard at first, but it got easier.

Coming out to a partner, significant other, or play partner can be either the easiest or the most difficult scenario to come out in. Your intimacy level, how open you are with each other, and the willingness of your partner to accept things are all factors in how the conversation will go. Some may have come to expect that you are into this; to others, it may come as a shock.

Here's how a sample conversation might go with someone that you're casually dating:

> *Olivia, we've been going out for a while now and I just want to let you know something else about me. I really enjoy it when you tell me what to do, when you hold me and we cuddle, or when you praise me. What I'm trying to say is that I really like it when you treat me more like a child sometimes and you act as an authority figure. How do you feel about that?*

Conversations with a significant other may be more difficult, especially if you have not discussed your intimate desires in a longer relationship. Disclosing passions and predilections is always risky, as there is some chance of rejection of what you consider a part of yourself. Many partners are willing to indulge or experiment however. For example:

- I never told my wife while dating that I was a bed wetter and wore diapers at night for protection. When we were married, I thought that I could go without wearing the diapers. By 6 months the anxiety was taking its toll and I was staying up most of the night trying to limit the possibly of an accident. I could not handle the thought of wetting the bed with my wife in it and was too embarrassed the talk to her about bedwetting and the use of diapers.

Well after 6 months of me sleeping less and less with her she thought that it was over and I didn't love her anymore. Talk about being cornered and scared to death. I loved her so much that I found the strength to tell her what was really going on with the fear of bedwetting. To my surprise all she said was, "You're kidding? Is that all!" and that night after dinner she escorted (more like dragged) me to the drug store and purchased some adult diapers.

To Friends

- My friends were supportive. One still wanted me to be godfather to her son.

- Most vanilla people that I have told really could have cared less. For most, I found a website (Understanding Infantilism) and showed it to them and said that that was what I enjoyed doing. I made it clear for most that I did not necessarily want to involve them in this, but just wanted to share part of who I am with them. I was very careful in who I shared with, and considered the risk.

- My best friend, who is also into BDSM, knows, as do a very select few other close, kink-minded friends. I keep these things private from my family, as I do not feel they need to know and I don't wish to tell them. The hardest person to come out about it to though so far was myself; admitting I had this part of me and getting my head around it.

Coming out to friends and family has a different dynamic and one may encounter different challenges as well. Since ageplay closely resembles childhood to an outsider, you may have to reassure them that it's not about you having a bad upbringing or something that they're lacking. You also do not need to get into specifics with friends and family, unless you want to. Generally, the broader that you make the declaration, the easier it will be for them to understand.

To Family

- I'm lucky to have an open relationship with my mom. I can tell her anything and she doesn't freak out. She lets me get tats and piercings; she knows I'm into the BDSM scene. And that my best friend is a 49-year-old cross dresser. Nothing really shocks my mom. If I were to explain my fetishes to her, we could chat about it and talk about it intellectually too.

- My accepting parents who did not accept that this is who I am was the first difficult thing I had to get past. After that, it was finding my place in the local community. I went to a local BDSM group and was not sure if I would fit in or if they could help me.

- I have told a small handful of people only a small amount of information about this, including my Mom and a couple friends. All were OK with it, but I didn't go into great detail. I still don't feel comfortable enough to just come out completely and say "this is part of who I am."

- I've tried to tell my mother, that didn't go over well so I played it off.

- I didn't tell my parents until I no longer lived with them.

- I came out to my daughters shortly after I'd found ageplay and they were very receptive of it and have no problem with my little side.

Many people appear not to have had too much luck with disclosing their ageplay roles to their family, especially parents. This may have to do with the intimacy, emotional connections, and possibly implications of child rearing. Once again, speaking in generalities may be helpful in this situation. Here is a sample statement:

> *Mom, I want to let you know something more about me. I like my boyfriend, Michael, to give more direction and guidance in our relationship. I like him to take care*

of making decisions and letting me know what sort of things need to get done. This just makes me feel safe and comfortable.

Not Coming Out

Choosing when or why to disclose your ageplay fetish is sometimes a delicate situation. You want to ensure that your coming out does more good than harm. Many people choose not to come out for privacy reasons, not to rock the boat, or because they don't feel it's important to disclose this information to anyone else. Here are some comments about why people are not interested in coming out:

- It's something that I would mostly keep private, because of the risk of people equating my appreciation for ageplay as pedophilia.

- LOL, well, my best friend found my fiancées locking pants the other day....oooooooooooook, so we just skipped that topic. I am sure she has her ideas. But no, I try to keep it to myself; it's personal and doesn't need to be shared with anyone who isn't into it.

- I would suggest that "coming out" isn't really necessary unless you are in a committed relationship. It's a hard thing to discuss if you're not interested in it. Some of my family members have inadvertently found my diaper stash. Others I have told (usually significant others). One Halloween I wore a baby outfit, and soon thereafter came out to some of my friends about it. For the most part, people seem to ignore it – especially my family.

- I no more discuss my ageplay with a friend or family (not counting my wife) then I would discuss ANY other bedroom activity. It is NONE OF THEIR BUSINESS.

You also want to make sure to come out to the correct individuals. In general, coming out to people who have no desire to understand or are not close to you is typically unproductive. Some of the reasons that people choose to disclose their roles are to find support, a sympathetic ear, or to assist those that are close to them in better understanding them.

- A few people. One was fine, another was good but later she betrayed me. Still another was seriously freaked out when I said I wanted to be a little girl... "Heh – you mean you want to HAVE a little girl!" "No – I want to BE a little girl." Yeah – didn't go well. It's always awkward. I would say if there is no real reason a person should know, don't tell them.

Others are intolerant and provoke negative responses to disclosures. Similar things also happen when people's interests are forcibly disclosed to others. This is another reason why people choose not to disclose or else use pseudonyms.

- Everyone has known that I am a DL since my early childhood – and being "OUTTED" was NOT a choice.

- Someone became enraged with me last year. This is not uncommon with me; I am very outspoken. Unfortunately, they were able to get my real information and they outed me to certain key members of my congregation. I was then outed by those members to everyone, and in many cases roomfuls of them got to hear one heavily bigoted side and never got a defense from me! I still believe the best defense is the one I used, which was, "I will not confirm or deny anything, as you will only twist it to vilify me. It really isn't any of your business – and you are sinning by spreading gossip."

Now that we have looked at disclosing your interests, we will investigate what happens with your partner after you acknowledge your interest in ageplay.

What to Do If Your Partner
Isn't Into Ageplay

If your partner is unsure about ageplay or hesitant to explore it, there are several things you can do to encourage them to join you in your fantasy. This section will explore some possibilities. Communication is a key factor. The first thing is to talk and discuss it with them, find out their feelings about it, and see if it is simply not arousing to them or if it is problematic in other ways.

If Your Partner is Unsure about Ageplay

- My first partner felt that I was only doing it for him, like fetishes are somehow innate. We broke up over it.

- Most of them took it well after some explanations, but I find that if someone isn't interested already, getting them into it is not easy. It happens but it's extremely rare.

If your partner isn't sure if ageplay is right or arousing, there are several methods you can use to work your fetishes into your interactions. First, explain your fantasies to your partner and field questions or misconceptions that they may have about ageplay. Realize that your partner may have some hesitancy asking and answering questions, especially if they haven't had much time to process or think about your fantasies.

Here are some questions that you may want to ask of them:

- How do you feel about this?

- Would you be willing to explore this with me?

- What sort of role might you see yourself playing?

- Where might some problem areas be?

- What part of this most excites you?

- What part excites you least?

These are some common questions that partners may ask:

- Does this mean you have a problem with my age?

- So why do you enjoy this?

- Does this have something to do with your parents?

- Were you molested, abused, etc. as a child?

- Is there anything else you want to tell me?

- This is kind of different, no? I'm not sure how to feel.

Compromise is often part of relationships and many people experiment with fetishes to please their partners. Many people have tried ageplay for the sake of a partner and enjoyed the activity so much that they've adopted it into the list of fetishes that they enjoy as well. Here are some examples:

- I came out to a few partners and ageplay friends. I showed my first partner a letter in Forum and said, "That's what I like." She ageplayed with me acting as Mommy.

- I was introduced to it by a Domme and was totally against it till I tried it. Now I love it.

If they don't object to it or seem to be willing to give it a try, you may want to try the following progression.

- Masturbate your partner while you tell them an explicit story or fantasy that you enjoy. This will introduce them to the concepts that you find attractive, while providing pleasurable reinforcement.

- Next, you may want to move to having sex while describing a fantasy.

- When you feel comfortable, you may want to attempt to let out your ageplay personality around your partner. They may have already experienced some facets of your ageplay personality. Slowly and gradually, reveal more and more of this personality to them over time.

- The next step would be to start to dress in your persona. Try little things at first, like hairstyles and ribbons, then move onto sexy versions of costumes, like schoolchildren or cheerleaders. If you are into diapers, then this would be the stage to start simply wearing them when you are with your partner.

- Depending on your partner, the next step would be either to engage in sexual or nonsexual ageplay. Sexual ageplay may be more reinforcing, giving them positive sexual associations with ageplay. However, nonsexual ageplay may be less threatening and allow some comfort with the role initially.

Remember that all people are different and process things differently. You know your partner best and should proceed according to your own instincts and experiences. Some people have discovered ageplay through their partners, found it enjoyable, and incorporated it into their sexual identity.

If Your Partner Dislikes Ageplay

- My Dom is squicked by it, so he's not a fan.

For whatever reason, your partner may not think that ageplay is acceptable or be unwilling to explore it with you. It's important to respect the wishes of your partner and not force your fetishes onto them. However, your needs and desires are still important and still need to get met. Individuals vary with how important their ageplay activities are bound to their identity. Depending upon the boundaries of your relationship, you may want to explore several different options:

- Focus on self-play: Many littles feel a level of satisfaction playing by themselves or allowing themselves to slip into headspace without a partner.

- If one partner isn't comfortable ageplaying with the other, they may be tolerant of you seeking another partner solely for the purpose of ageplay. This may or may not be limited to nonsexual ageplay, depending on your limits.

- Use other creative outlets like writing or crafts focusing on ageplay themes.

- Participate in local ageplay munches, parties, or other community building activities.

Other Problematic Areas

One group of people that may find ageplay problematic is individuals who have younger children. This group seems to be less inclined to indulge in ageplay. This could be because of the similarity of some tasks of childrearing and ageplay (for example, changing diapers). It could also be a mental block, as they may be worried that they'll think of their own children during play. One possible solution is to delve deeper into your role or headspace. Another is to choose roles, scenarios, and activities that are drastically different than your children. Due to the wide range of activities and scenes within ageplay, this should be fairly easy.

Another problematic situation would be where individuals live together, but for some reason, one does the majority of the household tasks. For example, if one individual cooks and cleans a majority of the time, playing the role of a mommy may be uncomfortable for them, since it is similar to their tasks in everyday life. Having your daily existence be similar to your erotic roles does not work for most people. It is called role-playing for a reason. If this is problematic, try role-playing tasks and roles that are dissimilar to those that are commonly found in everyday life.

Some people may have issues as well when playing with a partner with whom they are planning on having children. It may be troubling for a person to perceive the little persona in someone with whom they expect will be the parent of their children. For example, it may be confusing to realize that the future father of your children likes to be treated as a child. You want him to be mature, in charge, and responsible. However, he likes playing with Play Doh and sucking on a pacifier. The perception of both a father figure and a little boy in one person can be confusing.

The key to resolving the confusion is by helping the other person realize that everyone plays many different roles within their lives. In the example above, the future father has many different roles that he plays on a daily basis: a worker, boyfriend, son, friend, brother and lover. We do not act the same way for each of our roles and each role shows only a facet of our personality.

Adding to the Family:
Non-Monogamy and Ageplay

Marsha had a nice gig going. Babysitting was fun, easy, and it earned her a bundle of money. She always enjoyed babysitting nights. Mr. Anderson picked her up and brought her back to the house. She watched Tommy for a while, and when she was tired or bored, she put him to bed. He was always reluctant to go. However, once she started to "relieve his tension" in order to put him to sleep, he was much happier to jump into bed and wanted to go to sleep earlier and earlier, giving her more time alone. At the end of the night, Mr. Anderson would give her a ride back home. They'd stop off in a parking lot so that he could "enjoy" himself some. She didn't particularly think he was hot, but she enjoyed the job security.

Frequently ageplayers can have multiple relationships of varying levels and intensities. These additional relationships can take many different forms. In this section, we'll explore several different possibilities for these types of relationships.

Platonic relationships between ageplayers are quite common. For instance, if a little girl has several different friends with whom she ageplays, she could relate to each of them in a different fashion. One could be a sister, the other a best friend, and another simply a playmate.

Although not as common, other intimate or sexual relationships could be part of the family dynamics. These additional relationships could be ideal for polyamourous or non-monogamous individuals or couples and offer additional opportunities for play. A Daddy could play and/or be sexual with several littles who all play the daughter role, although they would not necessarily relate to each other as sisters. An ageplayer who is a little bisexual boy could have a mother figure, a friend, a sister, and an uncle, all or some of which are sexual with the little in some fashion. The mother, friend, sister, and uncle figures may or may not play together and/or be sexual with each other as well.

Multiple relationships are not for everyone. Many people see ageplay as something very special and personal and only engage in it with a certain individual or certain individuals. As always, where relationships are concerned, it is important to talk through what you both want and need. Next, we will talk about finding other people to play with.

Finding a Partner

- Well it makes it hard on relationships to have something that is so out there in terms of an interest. It restricts your dating pool somewhat.

- Finding a partner is difficult enough as it is without throwing my fetishes into the mix. But that does not sway me or make me feel inferior or anything. It just means I have to work a little harder.

- It's a challenge finding the right girl to fit into the age (role that) I like.

- The biggest challenge for a male is finding a female DL who will admit this very private sensual interest and be willing to share it within an adult love relationship – it is a very self-protected place.

- I also find it much harder to find ageplay opportunities than other kink opportunities, because I find most littles tend to want more stable relationships to explore their play, by and large, than many other kinds of kink, and the play I often engage in with those for whom my play is more transient tends to be quicker and more platonic.

Once an individual decides that they are into ageplay, usually they wish to find a partner with whom to plan scenes and explore fantasies. This search can take place both online and in person, possibly at the same time. This section will deal with some of the difficulties and offer suggestions on how to proceed with your search.

Remember, it may be difficult to find play partners or individuals that are interested in ageplay. Realize that it may take some time and digging to find someone else who shares your interests. Only a fraction of the population identifies and embraces their kinky sides. Beyond that, only a small percentage of those individuals identify as being into ageplay or related fetishes. Furthermore, you then need to take into account gender, location, age range, and personal compatibility. This could possibly leave few people who would fit into what you are looking for, so do not get discouraged if you cannot find your dream partner right away. Keep on looking.

There is a large disparity between the numbers of littles in the scene and the number of bigs. There are many more littles in the community than there are bigs. This could be for several different reasons. Primarily, more individuals are looking to cast off their responsibilities and act like children again than are willing to undertake more responsibilities in a play environment. When people engage in sexual types of play, they are often looking for relaxation and release, not managing others and responsibilities. Secondly, everyone has been a child at one point and can draw on those experiences, verses extrapolating what a caregiver role would be.

Posting an Ad Online

Starting with a goal of finding a relationship online may not be the best jumping off point. You may be better off finding someone who is interested in the same dynamics that you are, a friend or email partner, and see if things click enough for a relationship to form. Saying something like "looking for a friendship or pen pal, but if things work, would be interested in play or a possible relationship" may be a better start and get more responses than someone who is only interested in a relationship. It is wonderful meeting people with similar interests, even if the chemistry is not there for a relationship. After all, you never know if someone may grow into a relationship, even if they were not necessarily looking for one.

You need to prepare and plan prior to placing your ad online. First, identify appropriate forums for ageplay ads. You can find some relevant sites in the

Resources section at the end of the book. Before posting your ad, make sure that your profile is readable, grammatically correct, and fully filled out. Also, make sure that you have at least one picture of yourself. This picture should be a picture of you, with at least part of your body showing, although for privacy reasons, you may want to obscure your face or other identifying markings.

When writing your ad, try to make your post not too long and not too short. It should be about a paragraph long and give a general idea of what you are looking for. Remember to use proper grammar. This ad is the only way that people will start to know you, besides whatever other information you have posted. Neither giving too little information nor turning what you are looking for into a long-winded rant is desirable. After all, relationships require input and compromise from both people.

Post only in the appropriate forums when putting up your ads looking for a partner. Also, please refrain from cross posting your ad everywhere possible. It simply makes you look desperate and decreases the chances that people will respond, since it seems like you are looking for anyone, not a special someone.

When you get replies to your ad, take your time and read the email. You do not need to reply right away. Review their profile, and then, if possible, look at what the other things the person has written or commented. This will help you see some of their thought processes, likes, dislikes, and possibly help you measure compatibility. From here, just try to be a decent, sane person in replying and getting to know the other person (people) better. Follow your instincts.

Next, let's look at several ads, some good and some bad.

Ads Which Could use Improvement

These are examples of ads that are not ideal. They are inspired by real ads, but modified to avoid identifiable details. The originals were unedited as well and were not much different than what is shown here.

- I am looking for a little boy to fulfill my every desire.

- 36-year-old white daddy looking for my little girl.looking to wash dress taste hold lick love

- 46/m Dom/Daddy in the San Francisco area I.S.O. Fem sub

- im in Iowa and i need an attractive daddy ... im all alone and im a little girl

- I'm looking to be someones precious little girl. Im looking for a daddy 30 and below. Im looking for a daddy to love me and diaper me in real life. I want my daddy to dress me sometimes, change my diapers , give me baths (and sometimes take them with me), and teach me about my lady parts.

- hi, im 38 and live in San Diego. its my dream to be adopted by someone and become thier baby!! id do ANYTHING!!!! any help would be amazing so feel free to message me whenever.

- Ireland 49-year-old little girl looking for a dom daddy

- hello daddy dom seeking a online daughter

Although some of their content is oriented in the right direction, they do not include enough details. While not being overly specific, you can still provide details such as the general distance that you are seeking, activities that you like to engage in or more details about what sort of an interaction that you desire. Also adding a bit of detail demonstrates that you are willing to put in some effort.

Once again, proper grammar is important, even for littles. Although some littles like to use baby talk, it is best to start things off with regular language and negotiate from there.

Better Ads

These are examples of ads that are better or have some aspects of ideal ads. They are unedited and shown in their entirety (except for identifiable information). They are inspired by real ads, but modified to avoid identifiable details. The originals were unedited as well and were not much different than what is shown here.

- 37 y/o mtf queer Daddy. Single, but not specifically looking; just waiting to see what comes along. Dom, sadist, caretaker, spoiler. I like uniforms and costumes. I'm very into DIY in all aspects of my life, including toy making. I'm very into "Daddy" type toys. I'm not much into bondage, but I do like to make people happy *evil grin* and mummification holds some appeal. I like brats, but I don't reward bad behavior and therefore I like brats who know when enough is enough.

- I'm a 46- year-old daddy dom. That for the mean time is looking fo a semi local litte for an online little. I am looking for someone that is in the age range of 21-30 (actuall age) 7-9 little age. Online I am looking at times that will be aranged between us usually after 5 (seeing how I wirk during the day). If your interested and want to know more feel free to read my profile. and then message me. I have Yahoo IM and AIM. Thank you for your time and have a wounderfl day.

- Hi there, I'm a Daddy here looking for a baby girl that needs lots of tender loving care from a Daddy that will always be there to make sure his little one is safe and loved. Daddy is looking for a girl that is either adult baby / toddler or a diaper lover. Someone that is younger then 25 yrs old and a girl that lives in Alabama. Anyway, if this sounds like something you're interested in or something you need (to be loved and taken care of) then I'd like to hear from you. Daddy has an over abundance of loving affection for the love of his life. For more information on me or what I'm looking for or what I have to offer, send me an message and I will get back to you.

- Hi my name is millie n im an ab. I just turned 26 yesterday but in the ab world i like to be the age of 3. I have been into this for 5 years going on 6. I am very into this and do everything a real baby dose. I am looking for a daddy, age n location don't matter to me. I would love to talk and get to know each other and one day meet. Im looking for serious daddy's only ones that really want an ab girl in there life. One that they can love, cherish, and take care of. I don't mind part time or full time i'll take whatever the dad is comfortable with i like to keep it 50/50. It's not all about me, dads have feelings to. I also don't mind public or just in the house, I do both in my diaper like a real baby but if it grosses some dads out i don't have to do both. I like us both to be comfortable. I just won't have sex or anything sexual what so ever so don't go there. Please read my profile and if any daddys are intested please get back to me. Thanks and have a nice day.

- I'm pretty bad at these personal things, but I thought I'd give it a try. I'm looking for a kindhearted, loving mommy or daddy, preferably under the age of 35, either in the NJ area or where you can easily get here. I'd like this to be a plutonic loving parent/daughter relationship maybe at first, but I'm very open to it becoming more if it comes. I am NOT looking for diaper sex or anything like that. I'm looking for a caretaker to take care of me in exchange for unlimited love and cuddles from a sweet baby girl. I am a 19-year-old college student, very short and petite, intelligent and with her own hobbies and such. Are you out there, mommy/daddy?

A better ad illuminates several different points. A well-written ad tells a little about you, what you enjoy, and what you are seeking. Once again, proper grammar and the ability to convey your thoughts and ideas are important, as this is what people will use to judge if they will respond or not. Good ads state a little of what they are looking for, as well as what they offer to a partner.

Mailing Potential Partners Individually

If you decide to go about mailing individual people, please first check and ensure that they are looking for either play partners or some type of relationship. Most people prefer not to be emailed out of the blue about relationships, so it might benefit you to get to know them a little better first. A suggestion may be to ask about the possibility about playing sometime or meeting up may go over better. Also messages that are cut and pasted, generically phrased, and sent to many people at once are less effective.

Finding Partners in Person

The best bet for meeting other ageplayers in your area is networking and meeting people who are specifically interested in ageplay. Meeting other people into the scene through munches, classes, and conventions is likely the best way to find individuals who share your interests. Other possible ways include participating in events, volunteering, and participating in demos and classes.

Many people are looking for play opportunities and are willing to play as long as you ask them. A lot of the reasons that people come out to events or seek friends or play partners is because they're sociable, want to meet new people, and experience new things.

Asking someone to play can often be a difficult step for many people, as there's always the possibility of rejection. Although it may be hard, try not to take rejection personally. There are many reasons that a person may not be able to or desire to play. Just remember that not all people are compatible, and that may be some of the reason that play may not work out. Other possible reasons may include: too similar an orientation (both dominants); different sexual orientations (homosexual when you're straight and opposite gendered); relationship restrictions (married and can't play or can only engage in play with specific genders or play styles); incompatible play styles (she only likes flogging and you don't do that); too tired or sore for play; or any other number of scenarios.

When approaching someone for play, remember to be respectful. If something works out, it works out. If not, well, it's not the end of the world. Always try to make your encounters positive. Even if play doesn't work out, you've still met and conversed with an interesting person.

Cautions

Just like in any other sort of partner situation, there are always a few bad seeds. Try not to be overly concerned about these negative aspects; simply be aware of them and keep them in mind. Not everyone has a correct view of ageplay, and people are able to twist and subvert some of the wondrous aspects of ageplay into codependency or abuse situations. Sadly, there are people who take advantage of others. This is not always the case, but sometimes, a disclosure that one is into ageplay might be perceived as an individual being codependent, vulnerable, or easily taken advantage of, or something else that makes the work of a predator easier.

There is also the issue of people claiming to be into ageplay, simply to find someone else with whom to play or connect. Some people are desperate or lonely and will claim anything, so use caution when appropriate. One solution would be to ask them what they find interesting or what draws them to ageplay.

Another reminder, when meeting a new person for the first time, do so in a public place. This way you can get the measure of a person, and if you have a gut feeling that something is not right, you are not obligated to stay. Also having other people around will discourage anyone from making a scene. Additionally, arrange a safe call. This is a predetermined check in time with a friend who knows who you are with and where you are to ensure that you're safe.

Now that we've talked about getting to meet people, we'll move on and speak about negotiating play.

Negotiation

- First, I had to be comfortable with the idea in my own head, which happened when I met up with a gentleman for some "phone play." We set up elaborate scenarios of Daddy and his lil girl, and the more we discussed specific details and relationship dynamics, the more aroused we became.

- COMMUNICATION. Always. And a solid starting relationship.

Since ageplay is such a wide topic, many people have different ideas about what ageplay entails. Each person is different in their likes, dislikes, and preferences in an ageplay scene. Also, communication is fraught with assumptions and misunderstandings. That is why negotiation is such an important aspect prior to playing. The negotiation sets the stage for the scene. Without clear directions, things have a greater tendency to be jumbled or not be as satisfactory. People can approach others for play or decide on a scene in many different fashions. The following is one example of negotiation that can guide your scene. This is not the

Be sure to set limits. I know of someone who was in little space and their "big" turned it into a sexual scene, and she did not want this, but as she was a little and she couldn't "just" snap out of it- she was quite traumatized. So between all parties- be sure to set hard and soft limits, and safewords, they are needed in ageplay scenes as much as heavy bdsm scenes.

time to be shy; stand up for yourself and state what you want or desire. Remember, it takes (at least) two people to make a scene, so being flexible and understanding is important.

There's also no power dynamics involved in negotiation. Everyone is equal in making requests or decisions. Both people have the responsibility to bring up concerns and address issues during negotiation. People should not be in headspace while negotiating, as this would drastically impact dynamics and negotiations.

Positive Negotiation

There are lots of different ways to negotiate a scene; however, keeping things focused on the positive tends to make negotiations and scenes easier. Most people have a variety of fetishes or interests, so one excellent way to narrow things down is to ask your partner for a couple things that they enjoy. This is known as the "Negotiating Rule of Three" and generally provides a good amount of information and allows a good starting point for further negotiation and clarification. Here is an example of how negotiation might go:

Randy (who is a Top and a Daddy) and Belina (who is a switch and little) met at a play party, decided that they were attracted to each other and decided to do a scene together. They retired to the social area and decided to work out what sort of scene they desired.

Randy: I think that you're very attractive and I'm really interested in playing. So what are three things that that you like?

Belina: Um, well, I really like impact play, I like being scolded, especially for touching myself, and I also really like having my hair pulled.

Randy: Well, that's great! I also really enjoy hair pulling and impact play.

This is also the time that you would want to discuss the tone and tenor of your scene (nice, mean, etc.) and make sure that you're envisioning a similar scene.

Belina: Well, I really like Daddy/daughter scenarios, what about you?

Randy: The same here. I also prefer something that's set at home. Also, I feel best when I'm authoritative and in control.

Belina: Yeah, that sounds good to me.

Hard Limits

Hard limits are things that you object to doing and people should not do to you. These can be physical or emotional acts. It is not bad to have hard limits; they're simply things that you don't wish to experience. It is hard to create an exhaustive list of hard limits and most rarely end up cropping up in scenes. For example, how many scenes could you imagine that would lead to your partner cutting your hair? How about sticking eels into your orifices? These are not things that usually come up when you think of your list. Instead of giving an exhaustive or partially exhausted list of hard limits, it is better to negotiate well, and if something looks like it's heading towards a hard limit, use your safe words.

Belina: I think you should know that I don't play with canes. I had a bad experience once, and I'm not ready to try them out again quite yet.

Randy: That sounds fine, not a problem. I can spank you, or if you're okay with it, use a paddle on you.

Belina: Yeah, either of those would be fine for me.

Disclosing Physical Issues

Since some aspects of play are physical, you should disclose any physical issues relevant to your body. These could be either chronic or acute issues. These physical issues could also be something as simple as that you're sunburned, sore that day, or any number of things. Other medical conditions, like having a weak joint or difficulty kneeling, are also important for your partner to know.

> *Randy: Just to let you know, if you're squirmy or resistive, try to watch out for my knees. I had one dislocated last year.*

> *Belina: Ewww, that must have sucked, I'll avoid them totally.*

If you are planning on having sexual contact, this would also be where you disclose when you were last tested and if you have any sexually transmitted infections (STIs), issues regarding protection, or other related issues.

> *Belina: I love giving oral sex and usually do it without a condom. When was your last STI screening?*

> *Randy: I just had one about two weeks ago and it was negative. There are no issues that I'm aware of. If we did anything more than oral though, we'd have to stop, renegotiate, and I'd have to use a condom.*

> *Belina: I agree. I'm clean as well, no issues here. We'll see if we get there or not, and if we do, we'll stop and renegotiate.*

Disclosing Emotional Aspects and Motivations

Many ageplay scenes involve emotional aspects. This area consists of all sorts of different mental and emotional processes that could be either desirable or undesirable. People have either positive or negative associations with certain words or actions. It is beneficial to share these with your partner at this stage.

This is where you should talk through with your partner to find what emotions and emotional tenor will work best for your scene together. It is important to have the right emotional feel to a scene and make sure that you are both on the same page.

This is also the time that you should tell your partner what sort of emotions or emotional triggers to avoid. This can range from a certain activity that brings up emotional distress, (i.e., do not slap me on the face) to words or language that that would cause negative implications (i.e. being called fat or stupid). Here's a sample interaction:

> *Randy: Okay, so when I'm doing the scolding, is there anything that you'd like me to do or not do?*

> *Belina: I'm okay with pretty much anything, especially being called a dirty girl and slut, but it doesn't feel great when I'm called lazy. So if you could stay away from that, it would be great.*

> *Randy: No problem at all, easily done.*

You don't need to disclose your entire life story in negotiation or give a lot of justification if you don't feel comfortable. If you have a limit, your partner should respect that without a lot of justification. Just stick to the relevant issues that could come up in a scene. If you start to feel any negative, unwanted emotions coming up in play, remember you can use your safewords.

Safewords

People often have safewords, or short words that convey longer meanings when used in a scene. Some events may have safewords that are specific to them. Traditionally in many types of BDSM scenes, people use red or yellow.

You can use *"Yellow" to* indicate that the scene should slow down or change direction. Depending on the scene, this could mean some sort of discomfort (maybe a leg cramp), a need to focus on a different part of the body (for example spanking one cheek too much), or simply that the person who safeworded needs a breath to calm and collect themselves. When you use this safeword, play should temporarily slow down or the intensity of your activity should decrease.

You can use *"Red" to* indicate that the scene should stop immediately. You can use this safeword to indicate that you in distress or that you simply do not want the scene to continue. When you use this safeword, play should cease immediately.

There is no shame in using safewords; it is simply communication. If you are not getting what you want from the scene, you should stop or slow down the action, communicate, and continue when and if you can find something more comfortable. Generally, bottoms or subs tend to safeword more often than tops or dominants do.

> *Randy and Belina are engaged in their scene when Belinda says "Yellow." Randi is still rubbing her reddened bottom as she continues. "I need you to lighten up with the spanking a little bit. It's a little bit hard and I think I need a little more warm-up." Randy replies, "Not a problem," and goes back to swatting her backside a bit more gently, building her up for more in the near future.*

When people get used to playing together, they may want to alter the *Yellow* safeword to be something more in the vein of ageplay, as not to break the verisimilitude of the scene. For example, in order to clue in your partner to slow down, instead of saying *yellow*, which would seem out of context, you may say: "Owwwwa!" Instead of saying red, you may agree to say "Stop Daddy!"

During some activities, you may not be able to use your mouth due to something inside of it or another situation that would render you not verbal (like deep subspace). During activities such as these, you should have some sort of method to indicate safewords. This could include holding a ball or bell and dropping or ringing it when something needs to be communicated. The following scene is an example of this:

> *Tina and Rafealo have been doing quite a number of ageplay scenes together. They are used to each other's play style and have frequently played together. During their scene, Rafealo is "forcing" Tina to perform oral sex on him. He feels three quick raps of her hand on his thigh, the sign that they agreed upon indicating "yellow." They pause the scene and he withdraws from her. She rubs her jaw and moves it around. "Sorry", she says, "it was really aching." After a couple of minutes, once her jaw feels right, they resume the scene.*

Aftercare

Realize that some people may need to be left alone during the aftercare period. This doesn't mean that they're rejecting the other person or disliked the scene, but simply need some time to process the scene and transition back out of their role. Negotiate whatever works best for you, since your aftercare needs are very personal. Here's an example:

> *Randy and Belina have finished with their scene and have retreated to a quieter area for some aftercare. Randy sits down on the sofa and Belina curls up with her head in his lap. Thinking back to their earlier conversation, Randy covers her with a blanket and strokes her hair. As they spoke about before, they just sit and cuddle and do not speak.*

During the Scene

During the scene is when all of the aspects of negotiation come together into play. It is important to remember what you negotiated for the scene and stick to that. Remember, if you need to go further, you can always pause the scene and renegotiate. Once again, there is no harm in checking in to make sure that your partner is okay, and it is perfectly fine to use safewords if you are having troubles or issues.

After the Scene

It is good to check in with your play partner after the scene. Generally, a day or two is a good amount of time to have processed the scene. Email, call, or check in with your play partner to see how the scene went, how they are feeling, and talk about what was good and what could be improved in future scenes. For example:

> *It's been two days since Randy and Belina's scene. Randy gives Belina a call to check up on her.*

Randy: "Hey, Belina, it's Randy. Just checking up on you to see how you are from the scene the other day."

Belina: "Oh, Randy, I was just thinking about you. I had a great time."

Randy: "Great, feeling okay? Anything I should do differently next time?"

Belina: "No, everything was great and I'm feeling fine. Like I said during the scene, maybe next time a little more warm-up, but besides that it was great."

If you need some additional guidance with negotiation, there is a sample negotiation form in the back of the book, which may assist you. There is also a sample contract, which may help you with negotiation or getting into headspace as well. Now that we have addressed negotiating play with a specific person, we will look at etiquette and protocol on a larger scale.

Ageplay Etiquette

Ageplay scenes are both similar to and different from other scenes. For example, similar to other scenes, you do not want to interrupt people while they are in an ageplay scene. However, the scene may be more difficult to detect than some other types of scenes. Obviously, people who are cuddling, engaged in punishment, or other sexual activities will be easy to identify. If you come upon a couple of littles coloring around a table, feel free to ask if you can join in. If an unsure situation comes up, err on the side of caution and ask as well.

Remember that simply because someone is dressed as a little does not mean that they are your little or open to any sort of scene. Some people either prefer to be left alone when they become little, to work out their own issues or because that is their preference, so do not get discouraged when they decline a scene.

Do not touch anyone else without their express permission. When meeting someone, you can always ask if they are a hugger, even when you are in little space. Some people are very sensitive about being touched and even a casual touch might be misinterpreted.

Clean up after yourself. Ageplay parties and scenes can be messy things. This guideline includes both thing from your scenes and personal items (like soda cans).

Ageplay Events

There are several different kinds of ageplay events that are held. The rules and expectations are different at each of them. This section will look a typical event of each type and talk about what one should expect, how one should look, and how one should behave.

A munch is simply a social gathering where people who are interested in ageplay get together and talk. Topics of conversation generally include some ageplay or kinky related topics, but other usual topics of conversation as well. These usually occur in coffee shops or in restaurants and are generally held monthly. People dress in ordinary clothes (at least to the outside observer). It is helpful when going to a munch that you are sociable to an extent and that you have a desire to meet with people.

If this is the first munch you have attended or if you do not feel as comfortable, identify the leader of the munch, introduce yourself and explain that you are new. The leader then should go out of his way to introduce you to folks and try to make you feel more comfortable. Munches usually serve to make connections between people for friendship or later play. Meeting other people into ageplay seems to be important in making more in-depth connections or scenes at play parties. Many people that have attended play parties talk about feeling more comfortable having talked socially with people at a different event or by knowing other folks. Some forward thinking munches have added a munch box, which contains small activities to do in order to bond participants and enable them to get to know each other better.

During an ageplay outing or field trip, a group of ageplayers will attend some outside activity as a group. This could be as wide and varied as going to an arcade, the zoo, a movie for children at the theatre, or any other activity that you could think of. These outings allow socialization and enable some to go into a positive headspace with others enjoying an activity.

Play parties are usually held in private homes or in adult oriented clubs. At these play parties, people often have different scenes and sometimes have play equipment (like a "naughty chair" or spanking bench) set up. Some of these parties may utilize a theme to bring the evening together, such as a Birthday Party, Back to School, Tea Party, or any other sort of theme.

Once you are inside the venue, generally you can dress as you wish, although each venue has unique rules and restrictions that you should follow. You are free to set up your scenes, play, and enjoy yourself within the space. Be aware that few places have private rooms to scene in and likely other party attendees will be watching you as well. Generally, parties have some crafts set up or group activities to entertain.

Play parties are excellent places to find play partners. It can be nerve wracking to ask someone to play, but if they are attending a play party, they most likely wish to play or at least socialize. Once again, if you are uncertain about something at the party, ask the leader or the host of the party.

Certain conventions or other events also have ageplay classes and tracks. Ageplay classes highlight and explain different aspects of ageplay and encourage you to think about what you enjoy or try different things. Conventions with ageplay components are an excellent place to meet other people into ageplay, network, socialize, and find play partners.

Afterword

Throughout this book, we have explored the many different styles and activities that people do when they ageplay. I hope that this work has you thinking a little bit more about ageplay, why you ageplay, and your connection with it. While researching this book, I did a lot of introspection, as well as becoming very interested in the different ways that people played, their feelings, and reasons for engaging in ageplay.

Just during the time that it took to write this book, the ageplay community has grown quite a bit. There have been several conventions, an ageplay specific podcast has been launched, and even now, a more comprehensive network of littles in the works. It is an exciting time to be interested in ageplay and I hope that this book starts further discourse in ageplay.

Works Cited

- Allen, C. (1969) A Textbook of Psychosexual Disorders. Oxford: Oxford Medical Publications.

- American Psychiatric Association (1980). Diagnostic and Statistical Manual of Mental Disorders (DSM). Washington, DC: American Psychiatric Publishing.

- Aunola, K. N. (2003). Parenting Styles and Adolescents Achievement Strategies. Journal of Adolescence , 205-222.

- Cross, P. &. (2006). Sado-masochism: Powerful Pleasures. Philadelphia: Harrington Park Press.

- DeGenevieve, B. (n.d.). Steven X and Barbara C (1999-2000). Retrieved 03 25, 2010, from Barbara DeGenevieve Artwork: http://www.degenevieve.com/sx%20media.html

- Diaper Pail Fraternity. (1992). Diaper Pail Fraternity Newsletter #62.

- Fetlife.com (2011) Fetlife Social Networking Site. Retrieved 3 29, 2010: http://www.fetlife.com

- Fetlife.com Most Popular Fetishes (2011) Fetlife Social Networking Site. Retrieved 3 29, 2010: http://www.fetlife.com/fetishes

- Greene, R. (2001). The Art of Seduction. New York: Penguin.

- Kinkaid, J. (1992). Child Loving: The Erotic Child and Victorian Culture. New York: Routledge.

- Kristine L. Slentz, S. L. (2001). Early childhood development and its variations . Mahwah, N.J . : Lawrence Erlbaum.

- Maslow, A. (1943). A Theory of Human Motivation. Psychological Review, 50, 370-396

- Pandita-Gunawardena , R. (1990). Paraphilic infantilism. A rare case of fetishistic behavior. The British Journal of Psychiatry 157: 767-770

- Phelan, D. T. (n.d.). Do You Know Your Parenting Style? Retrieved 03 30, 2010, from Brainy Child: http://www.brainy-child.com/article/parenting-styles.shtml

- Postman, N. (1982). The Disappearance of Childhood. New York: Delacourte Press.

- Savage, D. (n.d.). Savage Love. Retrieved 03 28, 10, from http://www.eastbayexpress.com/ebx/age-play-and-foot-fetishes/Content?oid=1547641

- Speaker, T. J. (1989). Psychosexual Infantilism in Adults: The Eroticization of Regression.

- Van der Kolk & Fisler, R. (1995). "Dissociation and the fragmentary nature of traumatic memories: Overview and exploratory study" . J Traumatic Stress 8: 505–25. Retrieved on 04 26 11 from: http://www.psych.utoronto.ca/~peterson/psy430s2001/Van%20der%20Kolk%20Fragmentary%20Nature%20of%20Traumatic%20Memory%20J%20Traumatic%20Stress%201995.pdf

- Watson, J. (2005). Retrieved 04 27, 2011, from http://www. phoenixnewtimes.com/2005-06-09/news/baby-man/

- Zimmerman, A. (2010). Attack of the Tall Dolls. Retrieved 04 26 2011, from Localnet360: http://www.localnet360.com/attack-of-the-tall-dolls/

Glossary

Adult Babies – Also called AB's. Adult Babies are those individuals who choose to role-play as babies. They may enjoy some of the following: sleeping in cribs, wearing diapers, being fed and changed, and eating baby food.

Ageplay – Ageplay is simply adults who role-play being a different age. During ageplay, some people will take on the role of children, while others take on adult or caregiver roles. Ageplay is simply a one variation of erotic role-play.

Bigs – People who play the adult roles in ageplay. Most Bigs are also Caregivers.

Caregivers – Adult figures who take care of and care for littles. This term and bigs can usually be used interchangeably.

DL's – Diaper lovers. People who enjoy wearing or having other people wear diapers.

Dominant/Top – These are generally the individuals in an interaction that take control or give orders.

Headspace – The role or feeling that one gets while ageplaying. It's usually described as somewhat dreamlike and very pleasant.

Littles – Also lils. These are adults who role-play children or babies. They generally play a dependent role in the relationship.

Safeword – A special word that is shorthand for either stop or slow down.

Scene (Otherwise known as 'The Community') – A scene is an interaction or series of interactions between individuals. These interactions don't need to be large or complex, but are generally erotically charged.

Submissive/Bottom – These are generally the individuals in an interaction that follow or obey.

The Scene – The scene is a shorthand way of referring to the alternative sexuality or kinky community. It includes the events, people and activities that are present within that community.

Vanilla – Situations or people who are not kinky or into the alternative sexuality scene.

Resources

Books

- *Toybag Guide to Ageplay*
  Lee Harrington, Greenery Press, 2008

- *Power Exchange Books: Age Play*
  Dr. Robert Rubell, Nazca Plains, 2008

- *The Babies (Photobook)*
  Susan Sontag, Powerhouse Books, 2000

- *The Age Play and Diaper Fetish Handbook: The Ultimate Guide to the World of AB/DL*
  Penny Barber, Lulu, 2010

- *The Mistress Manual*
  Mistress Lorelei, Greenery Press, 2000

- *Auntie Eva's Boarder (Ageplay Fiction)*
  Mako Allen, Lulu, 2006

Websites

- Kinky Social Networking Sites: People, Events, Discussions

  – http://www.Fetlife.com

  – http://www.diaperspace .com

- Comprehensive List of Ageplay Munches in the USA

  – http://www.Littlesmunch.com

- Understanding Infantilism - Ageplay Information for AB's and DL's

  – http://understanding.infantilism.org/

- Ageplay Podcast

  – http://www.biglittlepodcast.com/

- Online Ageplay Magazine

  – http://www.idiaper.me

- Cheerleader Uniforms

  – http://www.teamcheer.com

Ageplay Negotiation Form

Please note this sheet is for organizing thoughts about negotiation. You should discuss scenes and activities with your partner(s) more in-depth in addition to using this sheet.

How I should be addressed in the scene (names or nicknames):

_____

How I should addressed you in the scene (names or nicknames):

_____

Preferred Relationship Roles:

_____

My Role: Top/Bottom/Switch:

_____

Age or Age Range desired:

_____

Storyline or general idea of scene:

_____

Three Activities that I Like:

_____

Preferred Settings/Locations:

_____

Preferred Outfit for Me:

_____

Preferred Outfit for Partner(s):

_____

Three words how I should be treated:

_____

Emotional Tenor of the Scene:

_____

Language I'll Be Using:

_____

Language Partners Should Use Towards Me:

_____

Level of Sexuality/Acceptable Acts:

_____

Level of Aggression or Discipline/Acceptable Acts:

_____

Preferred Implements:

_____

Safewords/Actions:

    Yellow:

_____

    Red:

_____

Physical Issues:

_____

Relevant Hard Limits:

_____

Aftercare:

_____

Sample Contract

Although many people do not need structure that a contract provides, other people feel motivated, comfortable, and controlled by having an agreement in place. This also may be helpful for forced regression. This is a sample contract that you can use or modify to your liking.

      I _____ (your name) agree to place myself under the control of _____ (partner). I agree to stay in my role of _____ while my partner plays the role of _____-_____. The timeframe for this will be _____to_____.

      I have negotiated and consent to participate in a scene that includes (description of scene):

_____

      I understand that this scene will involve the following elements, acts, fetishes, or objects:

_____

I also consent to being punished by _____ (partner) should they think it is warranted. They are able to use the following means:

I solemnly agree to abide by this contract and stay within my role unless I'm experiencing true distress.

_____

Signature

_____

Signature

_____

Date

Sample Scene Ideas

School Scenes

- Visiting an older sibling at college and going a little wild (and perhaps some blackmail)

- First music recital, first dance recital, first school play

- Meeting with a guidance counselor who takes a power trip during the discussion

- A substitute teacher goes on a power trip

- The first day at a new school

- Child/teen doesn't complete assignments

- The first detention

- A visit to the principal's office

- A student is caught cheating

Teen's First Car Scenes

- Trying to 'trade' services with the mechanic or mechanic takes advantage of a teen

- First break down on the side of the road- stranger approaches to help for 'reward'

- Police officer offers an "out" of a first ticket

"Bad Kid" Scenes

- A teen/child is caught vandalizing

- Child gets caught breaking a window

- A teen/child is caught smoking, drinking, and doing drugs

- A teen/child is caught swearing

- Guard/officer and Juve doing community service

- Guard catches teen in shower at Juvenile Hall

First Jobs Scenes

- Delivering papers/doing yard work – coming into contact with neighbors

- A child starts doing chores and is rewarded

- A child/teen comes in contact with strangers during volunteer work

Religious Scenes

- A visit to the priest for confession earns a different kind of discipline

- A nun chastises a teen for her misbehavior

- Altar boy experiences

- New Sunday school teacher gets a little too 'concerned'

- Religious parents strictly raise a child

Scouting or Wilderness Scenes

- First camping trip

- Child works towards a badge

- Going fishing/hunting with Daddy (and his friends)

- First camping trip with Daddy (and his friends)

- Boys sneak off into the woods at summer camp

- A child is lost in the woods

- A girl scout decides she wants to sell the most cookies

Health Related Scenes

- First visit to the gynecologist

- A teen has her first period

- Teen pregnancy scare

- An adult needs to have the birds and the bees talk with a child

Friend or Peer Scenes

- A friend learns a new game

- Two children go on a treasure hunt

- A game of ghost in the graveyard gets out of hand

- A slumber party

- Kids harass other kids with worms and bugs

- A game of cowboys and Indians takes an unexpected turn

- A popular girl teases an unpopular one

Family Scenes

- Playing dress up and/or with make up

- Spilling Kool-Aid on Daddy's clothes/shoes

- Dress up ends in destroying Mommy's new dress

- Visiting grandma and grandpa

- Time with grandma and grandpa at the home/retirement community

- Spending time with a lecherous grandpa or 'grabby' grandmother

- Child tries to convince parents to get a pet

- A stepmother/father attempts to bond with a new stepchild

- A parent punishes their child for acting up in a restaurant

- An older sibling hazes a younger one

- A parent favors one child over another

- Sibling rivalry goes too far

- Parents try to feed their child Brussels' sprouts

- A lecherous uncle comes to visit

- A parent and their child have some alone time

- A stepchild moves in with a new family

- A child breaks curfew.

- Trying to persuade a parent to get a pet

- Being caught staying up late playing instead of sleeping

- A child embarrasses their guardian at the store

- A child isn't complying with potty training

- A child spies on their parents having sex

- It's bath time!

- Baking cookies with mommy

- Playing catch with daddy

Growing Up Scenes

- Choosing costumes for Halloween

- First solid foods

- First time eating like big girl/big boy

- Taking care of a first pet

- Lost cat or dog

- A child has a nightmare

- A child is unable to sleep at grandpa/grandma's house, hotel, etc

- A first visit to a haunted house, amusement park, carnival, etc

- Free ride is offered at carnival (or child/teen tries to get a free ride)

- Children play Doctor

- Child goes in for a checkup

- A misbehaving child gets in trouble

- A family adopts a child

- A burglar breaks into the house

- A child is caught shoplifting

- A younger child begs to go on a trip

- A child is caught masturbating

- Someone starts to dress too risqué or puts on makeup at too young of an age

- The babysitter is left alone to watch and put the child to bed

- A nappy afternoon

- A secret stash of porn is discovered

- A child really wants to go to the circus

- A trip to the park to play on the swings

- Splashing in puddles in the rain

- Littles watch a scary movie

- Sitting on Santa's lap provides an unexpected surprise

- Playing in a sandbox or at the beach

- A child is abducted

- Building a fort with pillows and blankets

- Picking out a book at the library

- Decorating cookies

- Story time for littles

- A child is trying to be adopted

- Your secret crush is discovered

- Someone discovers your secret journal

- A child star works with their agent

- Kids jockey for position at an orphanage

- A child is caught stealing

- A bully picks on another child

- An outing to the zoo

- A child doesn't follow the rules

- A child is allowed to pick out a new stuffed animal

- A child is called on in sex ed class

- A child gets offered a cookie for doing something

- A child starts hanging around with bad folks

- Coming home, someone interrupts a burglary

Romantic or Sexual Scenes

- Two teens on their first date

- An illicit relationship is formed

- You want to date a the star of the team

- Getting talked into having sex the first time by an older boyfriend or parent's friend

About the Author

Paul Rulof is an educator and author. Since he moved to Chicago six years ago, he has been active in their alternative sexuality community. He has degrees in psychology and sociology; as well as having a graduate degree that he perverts for use in the alternative sexuality community. He identifies as a dominant, as well as a Dom Daddy.

He is the author of the book *Ageplay: From Diapers to Diplomas*. He is also the Chairman and Director of Education for CAPCon: The Midwest Ageplay Convention. As one of the co-founders of the Chicago Age Players, an NCSF Coalition Partner, he is trying to increase the visibility and acceptability of ageplay in the alternate sexuality community.

He teaches classes, and throws parties that allow people the opportunity to both explore and accept aspects of their sexuality. His classes mainly focus on different aspects of mental play, emotional play, and emotional masochism. Always, his workshops are interactive, participatory, and explore the topic from different viewpoints. He is honored to have presented at DomCon- Los Angeles, Madtown Kink Fest, Kinky Karnival, as well as many other venues both nationally and in Midwest.

www.ingramcontent.com/pod-product-compliance
Lightning Source LLC
Chambersburg PA
CBHW072222270326
41930CB00010B/1954